The Pastors' Club

The Pastors' Club

Paul S Lyon

ISBN: 0996114807
ISBN 13: 9780996114806

About the Author

❦

PAUL WAS RAISED IN THE Methodist Church. He and his brother regularly attended Methodist Youth Fellowship. It was in the summer of 1971, just prior to his senior year in high school that Paul accepted Jesus as his Lord and Savior. Within a year, there were as many as sixty kids who accepted Jesus at the local high school. In 1973, they along with adults from Baptist and Lutheran backgrounds, formed a Charismatic Church and called it the "New Testament Church." Paul served and grew up spiritually in this church for thirty-five years.

Paul, his brother, Howard, and other Christian friends formed Liberation Suite, one of the country's first Christian rock bands. The band played and preached the good news in the western United States with "Christ is the Answer" ministries before returning to their home church in Texas. In May 1974 they moved to Belfast, Northern Ireland at the invitation of a local ministry. This was fulfillment of a call that Paul had felt for at least two years to minister to young people in Europe. Christian rock groups had already begun recording in the US, but he felt that Europe was untouched by Liberation Suite's unique style of Christian evangelism. For more on Liberation Suite and their life in Europe See Appendix A—Liberation Suite and liberationsuite.com

After the band returned to Texas in August 1976, Paul returned to Texas State University, where he finished his degree in accounting and became a CPA.

For thirty-five years, Paul worked for the State of Texas and various local governments as an auditor, administrator, and financial consultant. During these years, he served as worship leader and elder in the Charismatic church from which Liberation Suite was sent out in 1974. After retirement, he formed Stafford Consulting Inc.

He and his wife, Daryl, married in 1983. They have raised four wonderful children and now attend a denominational, Pastor-led church and enjoy its fellowship. Paul retired in 2014 and completed this message, which he had felt compelled to write about for so many years.

Contents

Foreword

I COULD HAVE ASKED A number of men to write this foreword for me. However, since this topic is so controversial, and since most of the men I would have asked are Pastors or former Pastors, I felt it would have been unfair of me to ask them. Therefore, I have asked my wife, who knows me better than anyone else, to write this foreword. She and my three older children have read my drafts and have given me their honest opinions.

Paul Lyon

In our almost thirty-two years of marriage, I have watched Paul's passion for God's Word increase almost daily. He loves the Church and has instilled this love in our children through example and encouragement. Paul understands the importance of regular attendance, committed tithing, and reasonable involvement in a local body. He has studied the topic of church government for over seventeen years. This book comes out of a desire to see the local church function as it should: becoming a strong force in the community and a place where believers can thrive.

Daryl Alene Lyon

Preface

❧

My INTENT IS TO OPEN the eyes of men and women who have been taught that the local church is to be overseen by one man. I want them to hear about a different plan of church government. This plan and principles of church leadership are discussed by Jesus, John, Paul and Peter in the New Testament; yet rarely taught by today's religious hierarchy.

Many of my friends are Pastors. They and many like them are good, dedicated Christians. I have waited many years to write this book, partly to prove to myself that the message is needed and partly to consider the impact it could have on people I love and respect. It is fair to say that these people may be unhappy with the content presented in this book, to say the least. Nevertheless, I would have always felt disobedient had I not published this book so you can know the truth.

WHY I WROTE THIS BOOK

Why? Because it is needed. Mother Theresa, in response to the question of why she spent her life working among the poorest of India's poor, said the "need" is God's calling. I agree. However, in some cases, we should wait to embark on a project, even if there appears to be a compelling need.

I have known about these principles of church government since prior to 1998, and I felt compelled to write at that time. Because this topic is so volatile, however, I knew I must be certain that the Father wanted me to deliver this message. Jesus told parables about counting the cost before committing to a task. One parable was about building a house and the other about going to war. I am well aware of the opposition that will arise against this message—and maybe against me personally. Pastors and priests hold the most powerful positions in Christendom. Many will not abdicate their positions under any circumstances; others will do so only after they have challenged this message and found it to be true.

When prophets told Joseph and Mary who their son was going to be, the scripture says Mary "pondered these things in her heart."[1] I too pondered for all these years whether I should write this book. During the ensuing seventeen years, my conviction for this message has not diminished. That is one sign of God's calling. My thoughts have become even clearer and more certain on this topic. I am absolutely certain the time has come. I only hope that I have not waited too long.

This book is addressed to the church in America. Although I have worked with many churches in Europe in my early years, God spoke to me about the principles of church government during my time of leadership in Texas. These principles are universal, but I feel that this message should first be preached and taught at home. Where it goes from there is up to the Father.

REFERENCES

My background as a government analyst involved reading and understanding laws, rules, and policies of federal, state, and local governments and applying them to the governments for which I worked. These documents were the authority by which my employers were governed, and it was my responsibility to keep them well informed. Similarly, the Word of God, the Bible, is the Constitution of Christianity. Like the Constitution of the United States, it is open to numerous interpretations. Fortunately, Jesus told his disciples that after his departure, he would send the Holy

---

1 Lk 2:19.

Spirit, who would lead them into all truth. The Holy Spirit is the best interpreter, since he is the author of scripture.[2]

> But when he, the Spirit of truth, comes, he will guide you into all the truth. He will not speak on his own; he will speak only what he hears, and he will tell you what is yet to come. He will glorify me because it is from me that he will receive what he will make known to you. All that belongs to the Father is mine. That is why I said the Spirit will receive from me what he will make known to you.[3]

All the work in this book comes from my own study of the Bible and my personal experiences with Pastor-led and elder-led churches. I purposely chose not to confer with others or read scholarly writings on this topic. I normally seek to validate my work with numerous sources (pro and con); however, no preponderance of evidence from other voices will convince anyone. It is only the voice of the Holy Spirit that "will guide you into all truth." That is why I only reference scripture and refrain from quoting other people's "opinions." I did not want to be swayed by arguments for or against elder rule, and I don't want the reader to be swayed by people of letters on either side. I have presented my understanding of biblical church leadership as clearly as I could. That's why I relied solely on the Holy Spirit's guidance for interpreting relevant scriptures and my firsthand experiences.

Please read this book and the related scriptures with the same Holy Spirit as your guide. Search the scriptures as the noble Bereans did, to see if these things "be true."[4] Finally, he who has ears to hear, let him hear and act.

Paul S. Lyon
April 2015

---

2 2 Pt 1:20–21.
3 Jn 16:13–16.
4 Acts 17:11.

Overview

❧

THE PASTORS' CLUB IS ABOUT church leadership and how God intended his children to relate to him, each other, and the world he is calling to himself. It proposes radical change: a return to the elder-led form of church leadership. This is the only form of church leadership recognized by Peter and John and instituted by the apostle Paul and the other apostles in the New Testament. It more accurately depicts the relationship of a family. Many think of government as irrelevant to their daily lives. You only have to look at our federal, state, and local governments to see how government can impact us for good or for harm.

Most courts interpret laws by applying a *plain reading test.* That means the court first attempts to interpret the author's original intent for a particular statute based on how a normal adult with reasonable intelligence would interpret the written law. The whole reason I have written this book is because a plain reading of the New Testament clearly provides for the local church to be governed by a council of elders, not by an individual, whether you call that person Pastor or elder. To make a case for Pastor rule requires a tortured twisting and turning of scriptures, which clearly refer only to elders.

This book distinguishes between the gift or ability to *pastor* from the role of *Pastor* as a church-governing official. I use the *lowercase p* when referring to the God-given gift and desire to pastor and care for (shepherd) people. I use the *capital P* to describe the current elevated position of Pastor, which has no basis in scripture.

WHOSE KINGDOM IS IT ANYWAY?

Some Pastors don't care how small or ineffective their kingdoms are as long as they are the king. Seminaries teach young ministers that the Pastor is the ruler and chief shepherd of his flock and that lay leaders and associate Pastors are there to support the head Pastor's vision. Worse still, good men who try to use their spiritual gifts in a Pastor-led church find there is no room in the inn for their gifts. They give up trying or start their own churches.

Many of our "independent" churches are run like corporations. The Pastor operates much like a chief executive officer (CEO).[5] A church board, similar to a corporate board of directors, hires the Pastor, and the Pastor hires his staff. Other churches operate like religious versions of political governments, with regional, national, and international hierarchies.

New Testament church leadership was meant to be local and limited. There is no mention by Jesus, Paul, or the original disciples of a regional or national hierarchy to which local elders answer. Bishops, conferences, dioceses, and other hierarchies are inventions instituted outside of the New Testament teaching.

The Pastor role I just described places too much responsibility and authority in one man or woman. Even if one person and a staff could handle the job, which many cannot, it is not a role that was ever ordained by our Lord Jesus. For one thing, it institutionalizes a *false division* between brethren known as *clergy and laity*. This was precisely what our Lord and his apostles warned against.

Church members are as much to blame for establishing a clergy as are the men and women who occupy these false positions. There are always men who want to have someone do their work for them so they can escape personal responsibility. A religious hierarchy is an institution of man borrowed from political governments. It is an attempt to distance oneself from God our Father, by establishing an intermediary. Jesus is

---

5 Independent churches write their own bylaws and charter and select their own Pastors, even though they may carry the name of a denomination.

our only mediator. It was never intended that God's family, the Bride of Christ, would be run by a CEO or a religious ruler.

Jesus is our one and only high priest, our only king, and the one good shepherd. Neither Jesus nor his twelve disciples were members of the religious leadership of the Jews or even had formal training. He warned the disciples not to call another man "Father" and not to lord it over one another like the Gentiles did. When James and John asked Jesus to put them on his right hand and his left hand in his kingdom, he replied,

> You don't know what you are asking...whoever wants to become great among you must be your servant, and whoever wants to be first must be slave of all.[6]

THE FAMILY OF GOD

America needs a family. What we need is a church that more accurately depicts a spiritual family with God our Father and Jesus the good shepherd (pastor) leading us to the Father. Yes, we also need older brothers and sisters in this family to help teach and guide the younger ones. The elder model of church government most accurately reflects the family image.

Would loving parents designate a CEO as guardian of their child? Would they ship the child off to a military academy to be raised by the commander? Would they allow him or her to become a guardian of the state, to be raised by some soulless bureaucrat? God forbid it! They would ask their brother or sister to take their child into his or her home and be treated as their own child. They would seek a loving family; with parents they trust, to raise the child with their family values.

Likewise, God has not willed his children to a CEO, a commander, a government official, or even a religious official. He has ordained that his family be overseen by their elder brothers.

---

6 Mk 10:36–46.

THE ELDERSHIP PASTORS
AND OVERSEES THE CHURCH

The New Testament teachings of Peter and Paul recognize only elders as leaders of the local churches. Elders are collectively called to pastor (shepherd) and oversee the local church. The New Testament never mentions leadership by a single Pastor, priest, or even an elder. The only other church "office" is deacon. Elders appoint deacons to assist with church administration.

Elders are not hired professional Pastors. Elders are older men (*presbyteros*) within the congregation who possess the character and gifts to pastor/shepherd (*poimen*) the church as overseers (*episkope*). Therefore, elders collectively lead and shepherd the church.

There is no basis in scripture for a head Pastor, bishop, priest, or even a chief elder. There are no instances where a single man is referred to as the leader of the church in Jerusalem or any of the Gentile churches established by Paul and the other apostles. John, Peter, James and Paul never acknowledged a single man as leader of a local church. Each addressed their letters to *the church, the saints, the brothers in Christ,* or to *the saints with the elders and deacons.* Not one was written to a single man as leader.

Although Peter and John distinguished themselves by their gifts, Jesus appointed none of the twelve to a position any higher than the others, and none claimed to have such a position. The apostle Paul merely claimed that he was one of a number of apostles called by God.

GIFTS ARE GIVEN BUT OFFICES ARE EARNED

A gift is something given by one person (in this case, God) to an individual who did not earn it. A man with a gift to pastor may not meet the requirements to be an elder, and some elders will have gifts other than the gift to shepherd or pastor.

A position, or "office," of leadership is attained by one who meets the qualifications of the office. In this case, the office of elder is attained by meeting the requirements of character, experience, and devotion.

Elders are charged with shepherding (pastoring) and overseeing God's people.

Who Cares About Church Government?

Americans fought a war with England over its form of government. It's even more important to know and follow the New Testament plan for governing the Church—the Bride of Christ. So who cares about church government?

- Those looking for a church family care. Nonchurchgoers look at American churches, especially the megachurches, and see just another corporation with a slick front-man as CEO. How family-friendly is a government bureaucracy (albeit a religious one)?

- Men who have the qualities of an elder care. The professional Pastor role prevents leadership by the men who should be pastoring and leading the church. They are forced to choose between two sad alternatives: submit to the current system without using their talents or start another church, further fragmenting God's Kingdom.

- God cares, especially when earthly priests take the role of Jesus, our one and only high priest. A CEO is one thing; but priest and king are roles reserved specifically for our Lord Jesus Christ.

What Difference Does It Make?

What we preach and teach is important, but most people judge us by how we live. The form of leadership we adopt speaks loudly about what we believe. Two chapters, "The One-Arm Jesus" and "Churches on Every Corner," describe the pathetic picture of Jesus presented by today's church government. It is disunited and ineffective. It is ineffective because men with different God-given gifts and abilities choose not to work together in submission to one another.

Pastors serve in an unauthorized and exalted position, making them vulnerable to pride. It also subjects them to unreasonable expectations. This allows congregants to escape their personal responsibilities and place undue burdens on the Pastor. In many ways, the Pastor becomes a hired hand instead of a pastor. A true pastor-shepherd will die for the sheep. A hired hand will run away to another church when things get tough or he when he finds a better position.

When the Pastor fails, the whole church suffers. It is not the same with an eldership.

How Does This Work?

Some say that an eldership without a lead Pastor is impractical—it can't work. All Christians are called to a supernatural walk of faith. If we have trouble believing that godly men can work together and arrive at consensus on major issues, how can we believe in the virgin birth, the resurrection from the dead, and other tenets of our faith?

In chapter 21, I give an example of a church in England where it did work. Admittedly, it is more difficult for a group of men to arrive at consensus on major issues of direction, doctrine, and discipline than it is under Pastor rule. Yet that is exactly what Paul expected when he told Timothy and Titus to appoint elders in every church. He never once spoke about appointing a head Pastor or one elder or even a chief elder.

Why Now?

In chapter 28, I explain why there is an urgency to change. We are on the brink of a serious challenge to our religious and personal freedoms in the United States. Everything is up for grabs. We are no longer a Christian nation. We live in the second generation of Americans who do not go to church and whose perverted view of Christianity is derived from movies, television, and anti-Christian academics. They have grown up not accepting the Christian principles upon which our nation and laws are founded. They don't believe that righteousness exalts a nation and sin condemns any people.[7] Though there are many good Christians in America, our government is becoming more and more hostile to Christian principles.

Churches wishing to preach and teach the Word of God will be forced to abandon the CEO form of church government and hopefully return to a New Testament model. This book provides a pure biblical illustration of God's plan for church government.

We cannot put new wine in old wineskins. The current system of church government cannot be reformed, because it was invalid from the beginning. It must be replaced. However, many will not consider changing. Some have legitimate concerns and questions. Others have a position to protect.

---

7 Prv 14:34.

Section 1—Read This First

I PLACED THE CHAPTERS "DON'T Split the Baby!" and "I Love Pastors" at the beginning of this book to warn against using it as a pretext for rebellion or otherwise harming the church. Heeding these two chapters is essential for having God's favor on anyone's attempt to implement elder-led church government. I give examples of my own attempts to implement elder rule and how I refused to cause a church split when I could not convince our Pastor. I admonish others to "do no harm" to the Body of Christ. Every person is responsible for his or her own use of this book.

No matter how much I think the modern Pastor role is harmful to the Pastor, his family, the church, and the testimony of Jesus, I love many of the men who occupy that position. Most are sincere and self-sacrificing. In this book, I mention my personal interactions with Pastors in my former church. Although they did not agree with my interpretation and application of scripture, I consider them to be men of God. They taught me and others the Word of God in our early years and mentored us to the degree that they were able. They still labor for the Lord today, and I am grateful for their influence in my life.

Not all Pastors have altruistic motives. I hope and pray that those who do will lead the way to scriptural leadership by stepping down and getting under the Master's yoke with other elders. If they cannot, I appeal to them to resign and let others do the work.

CHAPTER 1

Don't Split the Baby!

❦

King Solomon had to judge between two prostitutes who claimed the other's baby had died and the living baby belonged to her.

Then the king said, "Bring me a sword." So they brought a sword for the king. He then gave an order: "Cut the living child in two and give half to one and half to the other."

The woman whose son was alive was deeply moved out of love for her son and said to the king, "Please, my lord, give her the living baby! Don't kill him!"

But the other said, "Neither I nor you shall have him. Cut him in two!"

Then the king gave his ruling: "Give the living baby to the first woman. Do not kill him; she is his mother."[8]

Our God loves his children, and so should we. We must be very careful how we treat the children of a Holy God. We should never use this book or anything else as an "excuse" for rebellion.

---

8 1 Kgs 3:24–27.

BEWARE OF A REBELLIOUS SPIRIT

> Rebellion is like the sin of divination, and arrogance like the evil of idolatry. Because you have rejected the word of the LORD, he has rejected you as king.[9]

The prophet Samuel spoke these words to King Saul after he disobeyed the Lord's instructions.

In this passage, Samuel equates rebellion with divination or witchcraft. Quite simply, Saul chose his own way rather than follow the specific command of the Father. Our relationship with the Father is preeminent above all other relationships. Jesus came to reconcile us to the Father. Just as Jesus did, we should honor God instead of trying to take the glory for ourselves.

Saul was also arrogant. It seems that *rebellion and arrogance are partners.* Arrogance is "like the evil of idolatry." This is a direct assault against the second commandment, which is to reject idols. Arrogance means that we value ourselves more than anything else. Both sins, rebellion and arrogance, exalt themselves against the person and Word of the Father. They put the arrogant usurper in the place where God the Father should be. This comes directly from the father of rebellion, Satan himself, who once said, "I shall be like the Most High."[10]

THE REBEL CANNOT INHERIT GOD'S PROMISES.

The rebel wants to exalt himself. He will use any means to accomplish this. It is impossible for the rebel to inherit God's promises, because he is not interested in submitting to God's will.

---

9   1 Sm 15:23.
10   Is 14:14.

Jack Frost taught about the *orphan spirit*.[11] He said that many Christians live as if they have no heavenly Father. They scratch, claw, and strive to obtain for themselves the things they need: acceptance, recognition, and love. Frost said that an orphan will be obedient for a while in order to get what he wants, but it takes a son to submit to the Father, knowing that he is loved. Jesus made it clear that the Father knows our needs and loves us.[12] A rebel is an orphan who will not receive a son's inheritance.

The opposite of rebellion is submission (not just obedience) and the opposite of arrogance is humility. Jesus set the example for us all. Satan tempted him with rebellion, but Jesus had already been with the Father and had willingly divested himself of his Godly form to take on the form of a servant.[13] Rebels won't do this.

DON'T SPEAK EVIL OF THE LORD'S ANOINTED.

King David succeeded King Saul because he was a man after God's own heart. He truly was a son of the Father. He submitted to the Father as a young man, long before he became king. He was also submitted to the Father's flawed leader, Saul.

Though God had spoken through Samuel that he would take the kingdom from Saul and give it to David, David refused to lift his hand against Saul. David trusted that God would fulfill what he had spoken. It would have been rebellious for David to overthrow Saul, which he easily could have done. At one point, David could have killed Saul, yet he only cut off a corner of his robe. Even then David's conscience bothered him because of this act of disrespect. He said to his men, "The LORD forbid that I should do such a thing to my master, the Lord's anointed, or lift my hand against him; for he is the anointed of the LORD."[14]

---

11 Jack Frost, *Spiritual Slavery to Spiritual Sonship* (Shippensburg, PA: Destiny Image, 2006)

12 Jn 16:27, Mt 6:32.

13 Phil 2:5–8.

14 1 Sm 24:6.

The end does not justify the means. For David to overthrow Saul would have been no different than any other rebel. That would have set the wrong tone for his reign. David's ascent to the throne provides us with an example of how we must respect God's authority and follow *his* lead.

Never "Split" the Baby

The whole purpose of this book is to build up the church—the Body, the Bride of Jesus. God forbid that any of us would be guilty of harming his bride. If the leaders in your church will not listen to the teachings in this book, *do not take the issue to the church at large.* It is God's work to edify his church. Although a church split may occur, do not be the cause. Though you will likely be accused of rebellion, do not let it be true. If you have rebellion and arrogance in your heart, you are disqualified from bringing this message to your Pastor and other leaders. Examine your motives.

In the church where I grew up, the elders didn't function as elders, and the Pastor believed he had a higher role than the elders. The elders deferred to the Pastor on every important issue. When a question was raised to the whole group, their eyes turned to the Pastor to get his reaction before speaking. This was not just because they respected his opinion. It was because they actually believed that he occupied a position different from theirs and that it was their duty to submit to it.

After about five years as elder in my church, I realized that I had done everything I could to convince the Pastor and elders to function as an elder-led church. In spite of all my explanations, teachings, and even confrontations, the elders and Pastor would not accept, much less implement, the ideas I have outlined in this book.

During those years, I desperately wanted to explain to our congregation how God wanted our church leadership to function. Nevertheless, I never taught anything or preached anything unless the elders and Pastor first agreed.

It was difficult for me, because I felt that our people suffered from poor leadership and incomplete teaching. The Holy Spirit restrained me from teaching something without the blessing of the Pastor and elders. Otherwise, I would have been guilty of rebellion.[15]

It was even more frustrating when our Pastor invited our former Pastor to preach a series of sermons on church government. In the early '70s, this man had been the first Pastor of our church and had recently moved back to the community. As a new believer in 1971, I had looked to him as an example of leadership.

After his return, he and I discussed the issues in this book. He believed in a strong Pastor rule. He believed that God gives a vision to one man (the Pastor) and that God brings other men to support him in fulfilling that vision. He believed that elder leadership was unworkable.

With this in mind, I knew what his sermons would say. He never discussed this important series ahead of time with the elders. He may have discussed it with our Pastor. He may have even taught it at the Pastor's request. The elders never knew what he was going to teach, much less had the opportunity to approve or disapprove. Although I had been constrained for five years from teaching the Word of God on topics of leadership and church structure, this former Pastor was given the green light to say whatever he wanted without review or discussion among the leaders.

I was faced with a choice. My choices were to take the discussion public and "split the baby" or quietly walk away. I could have started a "movement" within the church, but it would have done nothing but split the church. Therefore, I knew that my time had come. I chose to walk away and let God do the speaking. I could not split the baby to prove my point.

---

15 There is a time to go against the leadership when they are teaching obvious heresy and false doctrines about the deity of Christ, salvation by faith, and other foundational doctrines of our faith. With one exception, I don't think that the form of leadership falls into that category. That exception is the false role of a priest. We are to call no man father. We have direct access to the Father as Jesus told his disciples. To require any mediator other than Christ is heresy.

You should not raise the issues in this book as a general topic of discussion among the church at large for the following reasons:

1. **Most will not understand the issue.** They have never heard this before, and for their entire lives they have been taught that the Pastor is the authority.
2. **Some will view it as rebellion** against God's authority (the Pastor).
3. **Others will use it as an excuse to rebel.**

This is not our battle. It is God's. If we truly love the church, we cannot be the cause of a church split. Therefore, be obedient. Take the message to your Pastor and other church leaders. It is they who will need to surrender to the will of the Lord and to one another. Then you can all teach the church together as a unified eldership.

However, if the Pastor and other leaders cause a split, that is a different thing. If you have acted correctly, you are not responsible. Significant revelations from God may cause reformations or church splits because there are those who do not want to change. They have too much invested. The Pharisees chose to murder Jesus rather than submit to him as God incarnate. From Martin Luther's reformation to Wycliffe's translation of the Bible to the Charismatic movement in the 1970s, all were accompanied by persecutions and splits; but we should avoid them if we can. This is discussed further in chapter 26.

CHAPTER 2

I Love Pastors

❦

I strongly believe that the role of Pastor as we know it is not one or-dained by God. It developed when men decided they would rather have someone else deal with God on their behalf—a priest for hire, a religious professional. It is a concept as old as fallen man.

From the beginning, this was not God's plan for relating to man. He provided no priest in the garden. He "enjoyed" walking and talk-ing daily with Adam. He spoke directly with Abraham and Moses. Centuries later, he invited the children of Israel to meet with him on the mountain after their deliverance from Egypt; but they refused. Instead they told Moses to go talk with him. God warned Moses that after the people entered the Promised Land, they would reject God as their king and would seek a king like other nations. They did so over the objections of Samuel and became like other nations, even adopt-ing their idolatry. They paid the price all the way to captivity by Assyria and Babylon.

Finally, God sent his only Son, Jesus, as our ultimate intermediary. Jesus reconciled us to the Father through his death and resurrection and now is at the Father's side as our only high priest. Yet, we still seek intermediaries. Most of Christendom still looks to the Pastor or priest as a mediator between them and the Father.

This false concept places burdens on Pastors that are too heavy to carry. They serve as preacher, teacher, counselor, administrator, fundraiser, evangelist, and oh yes, husband and father. This is a job description designed for failure. The New Testament model of church elder leadership offers a better picture of the Body of Christ and brings blessing and freedom to the men who currently serve as *Pastors* if they choose to truly *pastor,* or shepherd God's family.

MY PERSONAL EXPERIENCE.

When I was twenty years old, I led a Christian rock band called Liberation Suite to Belfast, Northern Ireland. This was long before rock music was acceptable in Christian circles. Nevertheless, the Lord opened doors for us to preach the gospel to many young people in England, Ireland, Germany, Holland, and Scandinavia. Many heard, repented, and now live a new life in Jesus.

Because Christian rock was new, I was alone in many ways in my leadership. Although, I had the blessings of the Pastor[16] and elders of my home church, they were not quite sure how to handle these long-haired rock musicians. Therefore, I was pretty much on my own as far as mentorship and direction.

After about two years in Europe, while God was blessing us the most, my leadership responsibilities and pressures became oppressive. There were about eighteen people associated with the group at its zenith. That many immature people (some with families) brought a lot of issues. I was an inexperienced leader with virtually no mentorship, and these real issues began to weigh heavily on me.

I wrote a lengthy letter to the church elders asking for help. Their reply was that God was letting this happen because we were playing rock music. They still were not sure that God was the one who was saving all of these kids at our concerts, but they were pretty certain that rock music was the cause of our trouble. I was on my own.

---

16 Our Pastor even sold his car so we could ship our van and equipment to England.

I finally reached a crisis point. Up to this time, I felt a complete responsibility for the actions of all eighteen of us. In addition, I felt an overwhelming responsibility to all the people we had ministered to and those we were trying to reach.

This burden of responsibility became overwhelming. I had always been emotionally strong and had never understood how a person could be so depressed that he or she would consider suicide. But this period of time gave me insight into what it feels like. My only escape was when I fell asleep at night. But the next morning, it weighed on me as heavily as before.

One day, the Lord reminded me of these words. "My yoke is easy and my burden is light." The question He asked me next put everything into perspective and gave me freedom.

> "If you are carrying a burden too heavy for you, whose burden are you carrying?"

The answer was clear. I was not carrying *his* burden. I had picked up something God *had not asked me to carry.* From that day forward, I began to experience the freedom and relief from "my" burden. The band eventually broke up, and I picked up the pieces to make sure everyone returned safely to Texas. From that point forward, I learned never to pick up burdens that don't belong to me.

Pastors carry burdens God did not intend for one man. Tradition says they must carry these burdens if they are to be a Pastor. This book clearly points out there is no such role in the church of Jesus. Today's Pastor role includes responsibilities belonging to church elders, teachers, evangelists, deacons, and business officers. This false Pastor role carries a burden that is a prescription for personal and pastoral failure.

Good men and their families are drinking a deadly cocktail of false responsibility. They think they are doing God's will, afraid they will have betrayed him if they don't drink the cup. Finally, they feel condemned when they stumble under the load of a cross not their own. My prayer and cry to them is that they experience the freedom I experienced that day in Europe. *Jesus called us to pick up our own cross, not someone else's.*

We lose many men to these pressures—young and old alike. I think it is Satan's plan to burden them with responsibilities not from God. Then when they burn out or fall into temptation, another is ready to stand in his place.

It's not the man that is the problem; it's the false position with its unreasonable expectations. Many young men who want to serve God think they need to be a Pastor in order to fulfill their calling. I can see why, since the Pastor has inordinate control over programs and ministries. Therefore, to fulfill his calling, a young man must either curry favor with his Pastor or become a Pastor in another church.

Today's Pastors are responsible for much of the ministry of God's church, and I appreciate that. Some have learned to delegate the work. Although the work can be overwhelming, it is not the *work* that kills. It is the *burden of responsibility.* Pastors have assumed responsibilities meant to be shared by other faithful men. I pray that this book will deliver many Pastors and encourage others (elders) to step up and shoulder their responsibility. Then Pastors, their families, the church and the Name of Jesus will be better served.

Section 2—The Need

How good and pleasant it is when God's people live together in unity![17]

By this everyone will know that you are my disciples, if you love one another.[18]

The true, believing church of God is described in the New Testament as the Bride of Christ and the Body of Christ. The symbolism of the marriage relationship between Jesus and those who have faith in his love for them is an example of one of the most intimate relationships man knows.

Another intimate relationship is portrayed by God as the loving Father of his heavenly family. The Father, the Son, Jesus, and the Body of Christ are one. Jesus calls us his brothers. Yet, what we see in our nation is a broken church family. The divisions are glaringly obvious. The image presented to nonbelievers is a fragmented Body of Christ. This is a misrepresentation of what God's family should be. Sadly, the church is fragmented and ineffective, partly because of its leadership structure. Finally, this fragmentation prevents the local community of believers from having the best of the best. We have settled for the *best of the rest* in each of these fragmented assemblies.

AN IMPORTANT CLARIFICATION
I do not expect that all churches should be united. That won't happen, and it shouldn't happen, because many have chosen "another gospel" and do not adhere to the teachings of Christ, the prophets, and the

---

17 Ps 133:1.
18 Jn 13:35.

apostles. The true church is composed of those who belong to Christ because they have accepted him and identify with him.

No man can, or should try to judge who is a true believer. However, the scripture is clear that a believer is one who repents of his sin, believing that our loving Father will forgive him because he sent his only Son Jesus to pay our debt for sin. To be saved, a believer must also confess and identify with Jesus.[19] Regardless, there is only one judge: God the Father, and only *he* can discern the intent and decisions of the heart.[20]

---

19 Rom 10:6–11.
20 Heb 4:12.

CHAPTER 3

America Needs a Family

❦

I never had such a vivid understanding of our heavenly Father's heart until I became a father. Almost my entire adult life has been focused on providing, protecting, teaching, nurturing, disciplining, loving, and sacrificing for our four children. This is my privilege, responsibility, and my joy. Our heavenly Father is all this and more for us.

> ...I kneel before the Father, from whom his whole family in heaven and on earth derives its name.[21]

There are millions of children around the world who do not live with their parents or even know their names. There are even more of us who are *spiritual orphans.* There are many spiritual orphans in church who do not know their heavenly Father. He loves, provides for, and, yes, disciplines us.

> They will see his face, and his name will be on their foreheads.[22]

A spiritual orphan is constantly looking for a family, a fellowship, or a place "where everyone knows your name." Many seek this fellowship from the regulars at the neighborhood bar or through social media.

---

21 Eph 3:14–15.
22 Rv 22:4.

The heavenly Father offers us *his* family. He has given us *his* name. We are no longer orphans, for we have a Father and a family. Our churches should reflect this spiritual reality.

The world understands businesses, governments, and militaries, but people want a family. We will not change our society until we introduce them to God's family. Most of our churches look like businesses, strict religious governments, or little kingdoms with the Pastor as the king. There is nothing familial about these church organizations. Consequently, many churches offer "products" that spiritual orphans don't want. Our society remains fundamentally unchanged. What's worse is that our *church members* remain fundamentally unchanged.

Jesus said the church is the salt of the earth, the preservative that keeps societies from rotting and stinking. He goes on to say that if the salt loses its saltiness, what good is it? It is then only fit to be thrown out on the street and walked on. How are we doing in America? *Are churchgoers affecting the world, or is the world "walking" on us?*[23]

Why are we desperately trying to emulate the structures of business and other earthly institutions while trying to produce spiritual products? Like wearing a suit of clothes made for someone else, the church is awkward and ineffective in using the methods of this world. In one of his parables, Jesus mentioned how the people of this world are wiser than the children of the kingdom in using the things of this world.[24] That's true. Let us employ the ways of God's kingdom rather than trying to create an image that really doesn't reflect God's family.

I'm not saying that we shouldn't use modern methods such as social media, movies, and music to reach the world. Heck, I was one of the first *Christian rockers* in the early '70s, long before that phrase was accepted by the church. I know some of these methods can be effective in the hands of believers who have the right motivation. Even though some Christians thought and taught that rock music was of the devil, we proved we could use it as a platform from which to preach the gospel. We preached to

---

23 Mt 5:13.
24 Lk 16:8.

many thousands of kids in schools and colleges, in streets and concert halls, in churches and bars, and through albums.

We preached, gave our testimonies, and led altar calls to salvation in the United States, the Republic of Ireland, war-torn Northern Ireland, England, Scotland, Wales, Scandinavia, Holland, and Germany (for more about our experiences, see Appendix A—Liberation Suite). However, we did not alter the gospel message. We preached the straight gospel of forgiveness through the sacrifice and blood of Jesus and led many to salvation through repentance.

> ...if the trumpet does not sound a clear call, who will get ready for battle?[25]

In a greater sense, the American church can reap the same harvest we did. This will ultimately result in the revival that our nation so desperately needs. But ministers young and old, traditional and unconventional, cannot change the message. It must be pure and clear, or it will be ineffective. We are ineffective when we try to deliver a politically correct gospel, which is a false gospel. The world has no use for organized religion, and I understand that. Neither do I. Many nonchurchgoers will respond to straight talk about sin and a new, born-again relationship with the Father; especially if they see us walking the talking.

There are many spiritual orphans out there looking for a home. I'm talking about people of all ethnic, educational, and social backgrounds. Unfortunately, many have taken up residence in religions, cults, and philosophies that promise purpose, but the "home" is ruled by a cruel "stepfather" instead of our loving and devoted heavenly Father. We must go out to the highways and byways and compel them to come to the Father's house, where the banquet is about to begin.[26]

Our call is tainted by hypocrisy when we don't walk the talk. When our band was preaching the gospel, I made every effort to make sure

---

25 1 Cor 14:8.

26 Mt 22:1–9.

that each member lived a godly life in order 1) not to bring dishonor on our Lord, and 2) to shut the mouths of our "Christian" critics, who falsely claimed that we were doing the devil's work and not living a pure life.[27] I was never more vigilant in my Christian walk than when I was in full-time ministry in a foreign country.

It is my belief that if all professing Christians stopped participating in pornography, the pornography business in America would die overnight. The same is true with the perverse movie industry we all decry but support through our attendance. I am not saying we shouldn't see movies. Seeing movies is one of my favorite pastimes; but we must use discretion. If we do, the industry will produce fewer perverse movies. Likewise, Christians have a terrible track record of abortion, divorce, sexual sins, and drug and alcohol addictions.

Let judgment begin in God's house. There are many voices in our society, but if we walk the walk, we will have people listen. Are they listening? Not really. This problem can be laid at the feet of our church pulpits for preaching and teaching a politically correct "gospel" that does not have the power of salvation that Paul described.

For I am not ashamed of the gospel, because it is the power of God that brings salvation to everyone who believes:[28]

Jesus said, "They will know you are my disciples, if you love one another."[29] We must show them something different. Just as individuals represent Jesus to the world, the church is a living display of God's family to the world and invites those in the world to become born again into *his* family. Churches that act like corporations cannot offer that.

Most assuredly, the church is a family, and therefore we should look at how God wants to lead his family. I am a firm believer in strict order through a chain of command in the military, but that is not how God

27 1 Pt 2:12.
28 Rom 1:16.
29 Jn 13:35.

sees us. Neither does he see us as a collection of investors and employees who need a CEO as a caretaker. He sees us as his children. Jesus calls us his friends, and after his resurrection, he calls us his brothers.[30]

What kind of leaders has God ordained for his children? The answer is shepherds (pastors), spiritual mothers, fathers, and even grandparents in God's family. There is no other effective option. The New Testament speaks of only two church government offices: elder and deacon.[31]

Since the church is God's family on earth, it is no surprise that Paul says that an elder should be a family man. In 1 Timothy, Paul says an elder

> must manage his own family well and see that his children obey him with proper respect. If anyone does not know how to manage his own family, how can he take care of God's church?[32]

One of the tragic shortcomings of our American society is the devaluing of older people. I must be in the minority. I love to hear the stories and wisdom of older men and women; especially those who encountered difficult times. Let's face it. Anyone who has lived to be old has encountered a number of difficulties.

Proverbs is full of references concerning the wisdom of the aged. However, many churches today want to hire a young Pastor who can "energize" the congregation. I understand that. In today's church structure, we place an undue expectation on one man, the Pastor, and that requires youthful energy. In fact, it requires more strength and energy than even one young man and his young wife possess. More importantly, it requires the wisdom and experience of more than one man.

Consider King David, who, shortly after defeating Goliath as a young shepherd, was anointed by the prophet Samuel to be the next king. It was about twenty-five years later before David took the throne in Jerusalem

---

30 Jn 20:17.
31 1 Tm 3, Ti 1.
32 1 Tm 3:4–5.

as king of Judah and Israel.[33] During that time, he was constantly on the run for his life from jealous King Saul. He also fought the Philistines, who frequently raided Israel. For seven and a half years, he reigned over only part of the kingdom. Through all his suffering and testing, David learned trust in God. Not all things worked as simply as they had in his defeat of Goliath. But finally, over time, he had become the experienced warrior and leader whom God had selected to lead his family, Israel.

To lead a church properly in the ways of the Father, we need men who are tested. We need men who have already raised their children and who have demonstrated the wisdom and ability needed to run their household. Age alone does not produce wisdom; however, experience provides a better perspective than inexperience.

Do not mistake humility for timidity. Many people who promote themselves are not the ones you can rely on in a crisis. I would rather trust a man who has been under fire and survived than one who is new at the game. That's why Paul also said not to select a novice as an elder.

He must not be a recent convert, or he may become conceited and fall under the same judgment as the devil.[34]

What Paul is saying is that if you put a new convert in a position to lead, pride may seduce him.

Listed below are some of the requirements for qualification as an elder. These are qualities the Father requires of men who are to look after his family.

- Older man
- Experienced (not a recent convert)
- Courageous and confident
- Free from addictions
- Not violent, abusive, or quick-tempered

33 1 Sm 16, 2 Sm 5:4.
34 1 Tm 3:6.

- Not greedy
- Humble
- Wise
- Husband of one wife
- Accomplished in leading his own family
- Good reputation with outsiders and the church
- A student of the Bible
- Ability to teach and refute false doctrine

In summary, an eldership is a much better representation of a family. Elders provide more diversity of perspective, which helps members find at least one with whom they relate closely.

CHAPTER 4

Churches on Every Corner

❧

O ne of the most distressing results of Pastor rule is its effect on church unity. By perpetuating separate "kingdoms," Pastor rule divides the church rather than unites it.

Occasionally, I drive along a rural stretch of road outside a major city, through poor areas dotted with farms, salvage yards, and other types of industrial concerns. Such a drive is not particularly pretty. Interspersed every few miles, I begin to notice something odd. There are small churches of all different denominations. Some you can't even determine the denomination because the sign is unclear or its name does not reveal it. One day it struck me how sad this was.

In one area where the resident population was relatively sparse I saw more churches than were needed to serve the people. Almost all had no visible activity—no cars, no people. They looked desolate. Of course, this was just my impression. I know nothing of the sacrifice made by each Pastor, who probably has a full-time job and he and his wife run the church with whatever time they have.

This scene is even more pitiful to me than that in urban areas where there is literally a church on every corner. On this road, I saw the stark reality of the effect of a man's desire to be in charge of his own kingdom, no matter how small the kingdom. Why have they not banded together? Why do they not share their talents to shoulder the shepherding role? Even if these Pastors can shepherd "their" people while holding a full-time job, they present a fragmented picture of Jesus.

Am I just inferring something from a distance? No, I have visited many such churches, and I have relatives that attend similar churches. In fact, while I was elder, I had the chance to propose something "radical" to one such Pastor.

In our community, on the outside of town, where there were a number of small churches, a young married man ran a drug recovery outreach and a church. The outreach was a branch of a successful and nationally known program that began in a neighboring city. The outreach seemed to be fulfilling its goal to help men kick their habits and remain sober with the help of God. I was impressed with their work, because at that time, our church was in need of such a ministry. We had a number of men who were destroying their lives and their families with their drug and alcohol addictions.

Our Pastor tried to handle each of these addiction cases personally and, in my opinion, was not qualified to do so. One reason was that he was a very self-controlled individual who to the best of my knowledge had never struggled with addiction. Though the Word of God delivers men from addictions, I knew that the Word is even more effective when delivered by someone whom the Lord has freed from his or her addiction. My thought was that this young man had something our church needed, and we had something he needed.

He had come to our elders seeking assistance with his church's problems. His church included addicts, their family members, and others. His wife's relatives partially funded the buildings. After a church split, the relatives sought to foreclose on his property. His true ministry to the addicts was working, but he wasn't very successful as a Pastor, and this foreclosure was threatening his ministry and his family.

I threw a stink bomb in the middle of the discussion with him and our elders one night. I asked him if he was willing to give up his position as Pastor and continue to help deliver addicts. There was a deafening silence from him. Likewise, there was a deafening silence from our Pastor and elders when I suggested that he "resign" his church, let the relatives have their buildings, and continue his ministry to the addicts as a leader in our church. We could help support him financially and provide the spiritual support and leadership he needed to free him from his distractions. This would make him even more successful at his calling, and we would receive the gift of healing from addictions that I thought God was offering our church through this young man.

Neither our elders nor this young man took the bait. I experienced the same grief that night as I had when seeing those separate little clapboard church buildings every few miles on that country road. It reminded me of the story of the rich young ruler who came to Jesus asking what he needed to do to enter into the kingdom of heaven. When Jesus gave him the answer, he refused to give up all he had. He walked away sorrowful. He was not sorry that he couldn't have God's kingdom. He was sorry that he had to give up *his* kingdom. Likewise, I saw that same sorrow with this man and with our elders.

We want autonomy and identity, even if it means that our people suffer. The men who suffered from addictions in our church left their families. While I was there, our church had no effective ministry for addicts, nor did it have any close relationships with churches that did. This is just one sad example of the effect of the personal kingdom mentality that is primarily perpetuated by Pastors.

CHAPTER 5

The One-Arm Jesus

⚜

T he church today is fragmented. It portrays a strange representation of Jesus to those who don't believe. In 1 Corinthians, Paul talks about the oneness of Christ's body, the church.

> For as the body is one, and hath many members, and all the members of that one body, being many, are one body: so also is Christ....For the body is not one member, but many.[35]

> If they were all one part, where would the body be?[36]

Paul begins Ephesians by saying that God's will in Christ was "to bring all things in heaven and on earth together under one head, even Christ."[37] He continues this theme in chapter 4 by saying there is one body, one faith, and one Lord. Then Paul speaks of the various gifts that Jesus "apportioned" to men by grace when he ascended into heaven. The Greek word *charis,* translated as "grace," means a generous gift. Paul completes this thought by singling out five particular gifts to the church. These are the gifts of apostleship, prophecy, teaching, evangelism, and pastoring (shepherding). Jesus apportions these gifts to individual men

---

35 1 Cor 12:12, 14 KJV.
36 1 Cor 12:19.
37 Eph 1:10.

by giving them the specific grace (gift) and talents to carry out the tasks to which he has called each man.[38]

Paul says the purpose of these gifts is "to equip God's people...that the body of Christ may be built up until we all reach unity in the faith and in the knowledge of the Son of God and become mature, attaining to the whole measure of the fullness of Christ."[39]

In chapter 12, I relate a story about one of my former mentors, who believes in a strong central Pastor. I told him about my concern that I could not use my gifts of administration and vision in our church because the Pastor and other elders believed those gifts were reserved for the Pastor. His answer to me was that I should go start my own church. I was sad because I had no desire to split the church further, which I could have done. I wanted to contribute my gifts to the other leaders to bring our church into maturity. Why do so many men who have *one* of these gifts feel they have to start their own church to exercise that gift? Paul indicates that *all* these gifts are needed to bring the church to maturity and "the fullness of Christ."

Many Pastors, usually young men who feel God's calling, start their own churches because they experience similar barriers to use of their gifts. Many are not shepherds (pastors) at all, but they think they must be head Pastors in order to use their gift. Unfortunately, they really don't have much of a choice because of the restrictive leadership structure headed by the Pastor.

Recently, I spoke to one Pastor who I think is a very good preacher. He told me he considers his gift to be that of a prophet.[40] I think he is right. Maybe that's why I am drawn to his preaching. Others are clearly teachers. Some are evangelists.

Why do these men have to assume the role of Pastor to exercise their gift? It makes no sense for the foot to be asked to function like a hand

---

38 Eph 4:11.

39 Eph 4:12–13.

40 Prophets do not exclusively foretell the future; they also can be used by God to rebuke the church or society at large when they are going astray and to encourage positive change.

or vice versa, but that's exactly what we have in America. We have Bible churches pastored by teachers, holiness churches pastored by prophets, and outreach churches pastored by evangelists and apostles.

One man as head of a church will always default to his natural gift to the exclusion of others. We should have churches pastored by an eldership whose emphasis is on teaching, fellowship, and nurturing. Then others with gifts of evangelism and the ability to plant new churches can be supported. In this way, all the gifts are in use within the congregation presenting a complete picture of Jesus in the community.

Without all the gifts of grace operating fully, these churches look and function like an amputated body.[41] What we are left with, at best, is a local church that presents a picture of Jesus with at least one body part missing. How glorious is it to present a Jesus who can't see, a Jesus who can't walk, a Jesus who has no ears to hear, or a Jesus with no arms to hug?

Why do we have to go to one church to hear good preaching, another for good teaching, another for good worship, another for evangelism, another for a welcoming fellowship, another for passion and vision, and another for learning to reverence the Father?

> Instead, speaking the truth in love, we will in all things grow up into him who is the Head, that is, Christ. From him the whole body, joined and held together by every supporting ligament, grows and builds itself up in love, as each part does its work.[42]

Anyone who has spent time in the military knows that you can have the best fighters in the world, but if the enemy can divide them and cut off their supplies, they can be defeated. Our enemy has accomplished that.

Compare what you know about the many churches in your community to the following passages concerning the church in Jerusalem:

---

41 There are many more gifts than just the five mentioned in Ephesians 4.
42 Eph 4:15–16.

They devoted themselves to the apostles' teaching and to fellowship, to the breaking of bread and to prayer. Everyone was filled with awe at the many wonders and signs performed by the apostles. All the believers were together and had everything in common. They sold property and possessions to give to anyone who had need. Every day they continued to meet together in the temple courts. They broke bread in their homes and ate together with glad and sincere hearts, praising God and enjoying the favor of all the people. And the Lord added to their number daily those who were being saved.[43]

All the believers were one in heart and mind. No one claimed that any of their possessions was their own, but they shared everything they had. With great power the apostles continued to testify to the resurrection of the Lord Jesus. And God's grace was so powerfully at work in them all that there were no needy persons among them. For from time to time those who owned land or houses sold them, brought the money from the sales and put it at the apostles' feet, and it was distributed to anyone who had need.[44]

The apostles left the Sanhedrin, rejoicing because they had been counted worthy of suffering disgrace for the Name. Day after day, in the temple courts and from house to house, they never stopped teaching and proclaiming the good news that Jesus is the Messiah.[45]

Notice the unity of the people and God's response.

THE BELIEVERS
- Devoted themselves to the apostles' teaching and to fellowship, to the breaking of bread and to prayer

---

43 Acts 2:42–47.
44 Acts 4:32–35.
45 Acts 5:41–42.

- Sold property and possessions to give to anyone who had need,
- Shared everything they had
- Met every day together in the temple courts
- Broke bread in their homes and ate together with glad and sincere hearts
- Were one in heart and mind
- Rejoiced that they were counted worthy of suffering disgrace for the Name
- Never stopped teaching and proclaiming the good news that Jesus is the Messiah

GOD

- Performed many wonders and signs by the apostles
- Gave them the favor of all the people
- Added to their number daily those who were being saved
- Gave the apostles courage to continue with great power to testify to the resurrection of the Lord Jesus
- Gave grace to work so powerfully in them that there were no needy persons among them

This was a full representation of the body of Jesus. The Jewish leaders thought they had crucified their problem (Jesus). In fact, they had increased it exponentially. Now, instead of one man proclaiming the kingdom of God, they had many acting as one, calling all men to repent. As they found out later, if they killed one, another arose to take his place.

This was no amputee Jesus. This was the whole Body of Christ acting as one, and the gates of Hell could not prevail against it.[46] Jesus told his disciples that unless a kernel of wheat dies, it remains a single seed. But if it dies in the ground it produces many seeds.[47] Jesus's death produced

---

46 Mt 16:18.
47 Jn 12:24.

much fruit and continues to do so. He told them that after he died they would be able to do greater things than he had done on earth.[48]

What we see today is an emaciated, amputated representation of Jesus in America. We covet our possessions, we covet our positions, and we covet our free time. A covetous people cannot inherit the promises of Jesus for a powerful witness. Not only do Pastors need to step out of the way so the Body of Christ can be united in power, so do each of us. Many of us must be willing to stand up as one to assume the many responsibilities of the Pastor so that all our needs are met. We are approaching the days when we can no longer survive without embracing all the grace gifts God has given us.

Yes, Pastors will have to abdicate the throne of their kingdoms, so that the leaders of God's church can take their place. This way all the gifts can be used together, and the church can be victorious.

---

48 Jn 14:12.

CHAPTER 6

Best of the Rest?

⌘

A single man in power, for reasons innocent or selfish, cannot share leadership with men having different gifts. In fact, he may have a harder time sharing with someone having the same gift.

A Pastor may be willing to accept that another man is a better teacher or evangelist, but it is rare that a head Pastor will let a better preacher take his spot on Sunday. However, that is exactly what Jesus and Paul taught. God the Father wants men to work together, preferring one another in love, serving and building up the Body of Christ until it is unified and mature. They are called to employ the unearned gifts of grace that Jesus gave them without concern for their own position.

Unfortunately, what I see, even in my town, is a community with a disjointed and impotent image of Jesus. I can think of five Pastors of small churches who each possess gifts that, if combined and submitted to one another, could turn our town on its head. They could be the best of the best.

Instead, one church has better worship than all the others, another has better preaching, another has a better teaching and children's ministry, and another has more community outreach. Another has a welcoming and accepting spirit. Thus instead of having the best of the best, we have the *best of the rest.*

Even the best of preachers would benefit from taking a few weeks off to be refreshed in God's Word and refine his sermons. However, if all five of these men have the ability and desire to preach every week, why not let them preach on more days than Sunday. By the way, the gift of preaching is primarily meant for evangelism. Why don't they go outside the church building and preach? That's what our band did. Even though we were young, inexperienced ministers of God, he empowered us because of our *availability* not our *ability*. There is no unemployment in God's kingdom. Jesus said the fields are ripe, but there are not enough laborers.[49]

Servant leadership by elders helps remedy this situation when they submit the gifts God has given each of them for the benefit of the church. Even the apostle Paul, who was in a class of his own, refused to claim a position higher than Apollos. When the Corinthians were arguing about which apostle was the greatest, Paul only said he was no less than the other apostles. Even though Paul started the church in Corinth, he welcomed Apollos to build upon the foundation he had laid. Later, he asked Apollos to visit other churches he had started.

Pastors should be willing to take their place among other leaders and not be compelled to run the show.

---

49 Mt 9:37–38.

Section 3—The Wrong Church Government

I AM A FIRM BELIEVER in the "chain of command" for most civil govern-ments and corporate entities. Yet the Father has ordained a different leadership structure for his family. He has ordained only one high priest, one king, one lord and one good shepherd. His name is Jesus. Jesus warned us to call no man father.

Most Protestant churches today think of a Pastor as the chief gov-erning official, in addition to being the chief caregiver or shepherd. Unfortunately, in many ways he or she is also considered to be the CEO responsible for all business activities of the church, such as fund-raising and administration. Even worse, some Protestant churches—similar to Catholic churches—treat their Pastors as priests to whom the people confess their sins and through whom they approach God. The prophets, the apostles, and Jesus himself clearly disagree with this view.

The New Testament teaches and portrays a local and limited church government. There are no regional bishops or national councils. The local elders pastor and govern the church and appoint deacons to assist with administration.

Chapter 11 in this section explains the Greek words translated as pastor or shepherd (*poimen*), elder (*presbyteros*), and overseer (*episkipos*). The purpose of the eldership is to collectively pastor and oversee the church. Though men with spiritual gifts to pastor and teach should be heavily represented on the eldership, *not all pastors are elders and not all elders are pastors.*

CHAPTER 7

Models for Governing

∽❧∽

I have been an observer and participant in church government since my conversion in 1971. Likewise, I have observed, studied, and served political governments my entire professional career.

Various government models are employed by various types of organizations. Businesses have one type of governing structure, and political entities have another. As you will see later, God's family has yet another. Some governing structures are better suited to a particular mission than others.

BUSINESS MODEL IMPOSED ON POLITICAL GOVERNMENTS

Early in my career in state government, Texas elected its first Republican governor since Reconstruction. Bill Clements was a successful businessman with no government experience. He had just defeated a well-known career Democrat. The Republican revolution had begun. Many conservative Democrats became conservative Republicans.

When Governor Clements took office in January 1979, I went to hear his appointed right-hand man give a speech. He echoed a campaign promise of Governor Clements, which was to run the state like a business.

Clements believed in streamlining government by cutting the fat, getting rid of nonproducers, and rewarding producers. Of course, this made sense to a successful businessman whose mission normally was to increase profits and stock values. Apparently, it also appealed to most voters who were familiar with business and didn't particularly like or trust government. I was one of those. I voted for and supported Governor Clements.

In my first year of employment as an assistant State Auditor, I received a salary increase of 7 percent along with all other state employees. The following year, we received another increase of 9 percent. As a new employee, I figured this was normal. However, in my next twenty-six years of state employment, I was never to see such an increase again. To this day, state employees have not seen those kinds of raises.

Governor Clements was a businessman. He knew that to hire good workers, you had to pay market salaries. He knew that government workers were underpaid, and he proceeded to correct that. His next step was to trim some fat, which he did. However, as the realities of government set in, he was never able to run the state like a business, even though he was elected for two terms.

Governor Clements was trying to impose a business form of government on a political government. Although he accomplished some good things in his first term, he had to change his approach. In fact, he lost his first reelection bid and came back four years later to reclaim the office.

Although Governor Clements was technically the closest thing the state had to a CEO, the office he held did not have the powers of a CEO. In Texas, as in other southern states, the governor's power is diffused among other elected officials.[50] He could propose a budget, but he couldn't adopt it. He couldn't even budget revenues. The state constitution delegated that job to the state comptroller. He couldn't regulate the oil industry; that was up to the Texas Railroad Commission. In fact, the

---

50 After the Civil War, the Texas Constitution gave the governor very little power in comparison with northern states. The purpose was to make it almost impossible for a Reconstruction governor to impose his policies. This was true in many southern states. Therefore, governing power in the state of Texas and its counties is spread between a number of elected officials.

lieutenant governor, who presides over the state senate, is considered a more powerful elected official.

Governor Clements quickly came to realize that he had to form alliances with other state officials to achieve his goals. He also realized that he couldn't treat all state employees as he had in his corporations. He had no authority to hire, fire, promote, or discipline any state employees, except for those who worked for his office. Therefore, some of the fat remained...and none of the raises.

DIFFERENT GOVERNING MODELS
The Form of Government Must Fit the Mission.

The Business Model with which Governor Clements was familiar features a CEO who hires and fires his own staff. This staff includes a chief operating officer (COO) who in turn oversees a chief financial officer (CFO), a chief information officer (CIO), and so on.

The corporation's board of directors is elected by the shareholders and sets policy. It hires the CEO and gets involved in daily operations only if there are serious problems. The board has authority to fire the CEO. When the board fires its CEO, most upper management also leaves, allowing the new CEO to hire his or her own officers.

Political Government Models are varied. Here in the United States, we have a representative form of democracy. Other countries have kings and dictators, and still others have a confederation of tribal leaders.

Earlier, I described the government model for most southern states and counties. City governments generally have more flexibility. Many cities are run by a city manager, hired by the council and given broad authority to hire and manage his or her own staff. The idea is for the city manager to run operations without daily interference from the council. However, city managers, like CEOs, still have to deal with interference from council members or directors.

The Military Model by its nature is a strict hierarchical structure where orders are handed down from the top. With few exceptions, officers and soldiers are trained to follow orders without question. This model is obviously suited to the nature of the business: warfare.

Religious Governments are foreign to the American mind-set, yet they are alive today in Iran and other Muslim countries. In fact, our forefathers rebelled from a state religion as much as they did from a monarchy. The king of England was not only the head of the government but also the head of the Church of England. Centuries ago, the Holy Roman Empire ruled most of Europe.

Many times, secular laws of these countries derive directly from religious doctrines defined by their religious leaders. In fact, Moses, Joshua, Samuel, and other prophets governed the nation of Israel prior to the coronation of their first king. As we will see later in chapter 10, God preferred this theocracy for his people, Israel.

None of the Models Described Above Are Appropriate for God's Family

THE CHURCH OF JESUS CHRIST, THE BODY OF CHRIST, THE FAMILY OF GOD

I have never understood God's heart more than after I married my wife and we had children. It is no wonder that God calls himself Father. Jesus, after his resurrection, called his disciples brothers. We truly are the family of God. There is no more powerful imagery than that of the father running to greet his prodigal son. Those who have experienced this personally can understand God's pain when we turn our backs on him and his indescribable joy when we return.

Parents don't want to leave their children to be raised by a CEO. Likewise, God has not willed his children to a CEO, a commander, a government official, or even a religious official. He has ordained that his family be overseen by their elder brothers. These brothers have the experience and love to treat God's kids just like they have their own children. These older brothers understand that they are not the Father; but the Father has appointed them as loving guardians and overseers to feed his lambs, take care of his sheep, and feed his sheep.

Jesus asked Peter three times if he loved him. Peter said he did. After each response, Jesus told Peter to "feed my lambs," "take care of my sheep," and "feed my sheep."[51] In chapter 24, I address the duties of an elder to oversee and shepherd God's people. "Taking care" of God's people means much more than just "feeding" them. It involves laying down your life as a shepherd or a parent would. The CEO, the commander, the government official, and the religious official won't do this. They are hired hands and will run away when the wolf comes.[52] *Only a family member will fight to the death for his brother.*

---

51 Jn 21.
52 Jn 10:12–13.

CHAPTER 8

Churches, Inc. (The CEO Pastor)

〰️

M any churches are like corporations. The Pastor serves as CEO and reports to a board of directors who are removed from daily operations. When the Pastor disagrees with the board, he is out, and the board hires a new CEO Pastor. The new Pastor brings his new staff including associate Pastors. This usually changes church priorities and harms continuity. This model doesn't look very different from the corporate world.

Most Protestant churches think of a Pastor as the chief governing official, in addition to being the chief caregiver or shepherd.

As we will see in later chapters, there is no church office of *Pastor*. Jesus never designated such a role. In fact, he warned his disciples not to lord it over one another or call any man "father." Paul clearly designated elders and deacons to oversee the church.

President Truman had a sign on his desk saying: "The buck stops here." This meant he was responsible for all decisions and that he could not "pass the buck" to someone else. This is the mentality of CEO Pastors. This is a misplaced responsibility, a burden not prescribed by Jesus, and a prescription for personal failure. When a CEO Pastor fails personally, his family, his congregation, and ultimately, the reputation of Jesus in the community also fail.

When Pastors fail, some blame the congregation for not supporting him properly. At times, this may be true, but in many cases, the opposite is the cause. Churches with which I am familiar revere and exalt their Pastors. This places the Pastor in an exalted role not designed by

Jesus or the early apostles. Along with this exalted role come misplaced responsibilities and expectations. This produces the failures that are so common among CEO Pastors.

I am not talking about evil men. I'm talking about *good men assuming a role God did not ordain or prescribe.* Pastors and their staffs are expected to

- preach once, twice, or three times a week;
- counsel parishioners;
- visit the sick;
- judge disputes;
- teach the Word;
- plan social programs;
- develop programs for singles, young married couples, elderly, youth, children, and those with addictions or other personal problems;
- raise funds;
- develop budgets;
- attend budget meetings;
- approve budgets;
- run a business office;
- administer staff;
- discipline staff;
- develop and encourage staff; and
- anything else that is needed.

Oh, and if the Pastor is married with children, he must be a master juggler who can also work in time for his wife, birthday parties, Little League, soccer, music lessons, etc. His wife and his children end up paying the price for improper and impossible responsibilities. It cannot be done effectively.

- The Pastor deserves better.
- His wife deserves better.
- His children deserve better.
- The church deserves better.
- The other leaders deserve better.
- Jesus deserves better.

Just as a new CEO brings in a new administration, so a new CEO Pastor brings in new associate Pastors and staff. More importantly, the new CEO Pastor brings a new *vision*. This new vision usually means that certain programs will be changed or abandoned and new ones added. Some will be emphasized over others because of the priorities of the new CEO.

A corporate board of directors brings in a new CEO to change direction. They like the vision that he or she has and they want that vision implemented in their business. This also happens in Churches, Inc. Even if the church board of directors brings in a new CEO Pastor whom they believe has the same vision as the old Pastor, it will never be exactly the same. Each man has a slightly different vision of God's plan and how to implement it in the local church.

Changing Pastor CEOs brings about a shift of emphasis that normally results in winners and losers. Those who formally had favor with the old Pastor now have to build favor with the new Pastor or lose their influence. This is no different from what happens in politics when there is a change of elected officials. There are those in the church who curry favor with the Pastor, just as lobbyists curry favor with elected officials. I for one am disgusted by this. Much of this pandering to the CEO Pastor would be moot if there were no CEO Pastor. In later chapters, I hope to show you, as the Apostle Paul said, "a more excellent way."

THE HIRED HAND AND THE SHEPHERD

I am the good shepherd. The good shepherd lays down his life for the sheep. The hired hand is not the shepherd and does not own the sheep. So when he sees the wolf coming, he abandons the sheep and runs away. Then the wolf attacks the flock and scatters it. The man runs away because he is a hired hand and cares nothing for the sheep.

> I am the good shepherd; I know my sheep and my sheep know me—just as the Father knows me and I know the Father—and I lay down my life for the sheep. [53]

The hired hand is concerned about himself. The shepherd is concerned about his sheep. The shepherd would die for them, like a father would die for his child.

Too often, Pastors are like the hired hand, especially in traditional denominations. They move around from church to church and job to job like CEOs, city managers, or school superintendents. Many times, the reason for leaving is no more altruistic than achieving more prominence or a better salary. In other cases, it's because they were "fired" or "let go." If the new church's Pastor search committee doesn't do its homework, it may pick the "Old Maid" from the old church's hand. Admittedly, some are fired for doing the right thing and being honorable.

The church family should be led by a group of capable, older men who shepherd the people. In most cases, they will be long-time members of the community. Otherwise, how could they meet the requirement to have a good reputation in the community? Just because someone doesn't have a bad reputation doesn't mean he or she has a good one. It takes time for the church and the community to get to know a man and his family.

If the church leadership is composed of elders, there is a greater continuity and consistency of vision. It's OK for one of the elders to step out of the eldership or move to another town. This will not seriously disrupt the collective vision and direction of the church.

Most churches have men who are qualified and capable. Yet they do not have the opportunity to fully function as shepherds of God's family. As long as the Pastor occupies the roles of CEO, priest, and king, the church fathers will not lead the family.

---

53 Jn 10:11–15.

CHAPTER 9

Pastor-Priest

❦

T he current role of a Christian Pastor or priest is a tradition created by man. God has always desired to talk with his people face-to-face with no intermediary, just as he did with Adam in the garden and later with Moses. He offered the same opportunity to his people, the Jews.

Our desire for someone else to speak to God on our behalf and then tell us what God says is *an attempt to keep God at a distance.* This desire for a professional (paid) priest or Pastor is one way to absolve the individual from personal responsibility for dealing with God directly. If we appoint someone to be our priest, we either give him a position of adoration that he should not have or we use him as a scapegoat to blame for things that don't go our way. Either way, it is an attempt to avoid personal responsibility for our own spiritual lives and that of the local church.

> For there is one God and one mediator between God and mankind, the man Christ Jesus, who gave himself as a ransom for all people.[54]
>
> Christ Jesus…is at the right hand of God and is also interceding for us.[55]
>
> …because Jesus lives forever, he has a permanent priesthood. Therefore he is able to save completely those who come to God through him, because he always lives to intercede for them.

---

54 1 Tm 2:5–6.
55 Rom 8:34.

Such a high priest truly meets our need—one who is holy, blameless, pure, set apart from sinners, exalted above the heavens. Unlike the other high priests, he does not need to offer sacrifices day after day, first for his own sins, and then for the sins of the people. He sacrificed for their sins once for all when he offered himself.[56]

In addition to being the CEO, many churches think of the Pastor as a priest through whom they approach God and receive direction. *Most religions have priests because they perceive there is a need to bridge a chasm between God and the individual.* **Indeed, there is a chasm, but no earthly priest can bridge it.**

The *Merriam-Webster Dictionary* defines *priest* as

One authorized to perform the sacred rites of a religion especially as a *mediatory agent between humans and God*; specifically: an Anglican, Eastern Orthodox, or Roman Catholic clergyman ranking below a bishop and above a deacon [emphasis added].

It is this role as mediator between man and God that Jesus and the apostles clearly do not associate with an earthly priest or Pastor.

When my wife and I were first married, she said I was like Jesus to her. I assure you, I haven't heard that comparison much in the last thirty-two years. Needless to say, I was uncomfortable in that role. However, I came to realize that at that time in her new walk with Christ, she needed someone to provide guidance. Her religious instruction did not teach her to expect a personal relationship with the creator of the universe. She quickly learned to direct her thoughts and prayers to the Good Shepherd, and he speaks to her directly.

---

56 Heb 7:24–27.

Jesus, Our Only High Priest

Since the time of Moses, the Jewish priest offered sin offerings and animal sacrifices of atonement first for his own sins and then for the sins of the Jewish people. John the Baptist called Jesus "the Lamb of God, who takes away the sins of the world."[57] Jesus became our substitute sacrifice *and* our priest. As our high priest, he offered himself as a sinless, spotless sacrifice. He died once for all men as a perfect sacrifice. He paid not only for the sins of Jews but for those of the whole world.

After Jesus's resurrection, there was no longer a need for a sacrifice for sin—even for the Jews. *The apostles and most of the early disciples, who were all Jewish, never instituted the office of priest in the church or of animal sacrifices for sin, because Jesus is our high priest and our perfect sacrifice. He is in heaven, "always interceding" to the Father on our behalf.*

Every man and woman can now appropriate the mercy of God by confessing his or her sin to God and relying on Jesus's sacrifice. This is a personal decision of the heart, known as *conversion,* that each man or woman must declare publicly. No priest is required other than Jesus himself. Likewise, when believers sin subsequent to conversion, John says Jesus is our "advocate with the Father."

> My dear children, I write this to you so that you will not sin. But if anybody does sin, we have an advocate with the Father— Jesus Christ, the Righteous One. He is the atoning sacrifice for our sins, and not only for ours but also for the sins of the whole world.[58]

The English word *advocate* is translated from the Greek word *paraklētos.* The meaning of this word is similar to a defense attorney, or one who speaks on behalf of the defendant. In this case, Jesus stands before the Father, who will judge all sin. He is pleading for mercy for each one of us. His defense is not based on our innocence (for all have

---

57 Jn 1:29.
58 1 Jn 2:1–2.

sinned). It is based on his payment of our death sentence by his death on the cross. He can be our defense attorney only if we confess our sin and receive his gift of mercy.

MOST PROTESTANTS SAY THEY DO NOT HAVE PRIESTS—BUT IN REALITY THEY DO.

The Apostle Paul exhorted his converts to follow his example, but he never set himself—or anyone else—up as a priest. Teachers and pastor-shepherds are highly important in God's church. Teachers and other experienced Christians, along with pastor-shepherds, are meant to guide, train, and care for others. However, even if they have the title of *priest,* they are not priests.

There is nothing wrong in seeking wisdom and counsel from older and wiser believers. In fact, the Old and New Testaments encourage this. What is wrong is the belief that *another man or woman is your mediator to and from God.* No believer needs to go through a mediator to confess sin, to be forgiven of sins, or to hear from God. The Father, Son, and Holy Spirit commune directly with the believer. To set oneself up in Jesus's place as a mediator to the Father is an unholy place to be.

Some Christian churches, including Charismatics and other Bible-believing evangelicals, treat their Pastors as priests (mediators between the people and God). They establish a division between clergy and laity. Some literally teach people to confess their sins to the Pastor and ask him to pray for them. Others are taught to receive direction for their lives from the Pastor-priest, rather than seeking God's guidance personally. Although most Protestant churches do not overtly teach these things, the actions of the Pastor and the people they lead speak louder than words.

This dependence on another man for our own spiritual life is as old as man himself. It is an attempt to keep God at a distance and to blame someone else when we don't get the results we want. God clearly states that each man is responsible for his own spiritual life.

From the Beginning, God Planned to Have a Direct Relationship with Us.

Genesis 2 clearly states that God interacted face-to-face regularly with Adam. Adam and Eve were both naked and felt no shame before each other or God.

On the day Adam and Eve sinned, God came looking for Adam; but he was hiding.

> Then the man and his wife heard the sound of the LORD God as he was walking in the garden in the cool of the day, and they hid from the LORD God among the trees of the garden.[59]

Although God did not speak face-to-face with man after that, it was still his desire to have a direct relationship with each person.

Fallen Man and Priests

After the fall of Adam, it has been the nature of *sinful* man to want someone else to speak to God on his behalf. Man's first response is to hide from God's voice. Before Adam sinned, he and God walked and talked in complete harmony. In fact, Adam walked literally and psychologically naked before God in complete innocence. That was how God wanted it. However, after his sin, Adam hid himself when God called him. Compare this with the response of the children of Israel to God's voice.

Moses encountered God in a way that no other man since Adam had. He walked and talked with God daily. God revealed his plans to Moses, and Moses interceded for the people of Israel. Yet God wanted more. His plan was that the children of Israel would be a "kingdom of priests and a holy nation." In order for that to be, they would need to meet God and converse with him as Moses and Adam had.

---

59 Gn 3:8.

Then Moses went up to God, and the LORD called to him from the mountain and said, "This is what you are to say to the house of Jacob and what you are to tell the people of Israel: 'You yourselves have seen what I did to Egypt, and how I carried you on eagles' wings and brought you to myself. Now if you obey me fully and keep my covenant, then out of all nations you will be my treasured possession. Although the whole earth is mine, you will be for me a kingdom of priests and a holy nation.' These are the words you are to speak to the Israelites."[60]

Then Moses led the people out of the camp to meet with God, and they stood at the foot of the mountain. Mount Sinai was covered with smoke, because the LORD descended on it in fire. The smoke billowed up from it like smoke from a furnace, the whole mountain trembled violently, and the sound of the trumpet grew louder and louder. Then Moses spoke and the voice of God answered him.[61]

When the people saw the thunder and lightning and heard the trumpet and saw the mountain in smoke, they trembled with fear. They stayed at a distance and said to Moses, "Speak to us yourself and we will listen. But do not have God speak to us or we will die." Moses said to the people, "Do not be afraid. God has come to test you, so that the fear of God will be with you to keep you from sinning." The people remained at a distance, while Moses approached the thick darkness where God was.[62]

God was offering each one of them a relationship where they would be able to hear God speak directly to them like he did with Moses. Why would the children of Israel reject such an offer by the God of the universe? The answer is sin and unbelief, the same thing that separated Adam from God.

---

60 Ex 19:3–6.
61 Ex 19:16–19.
62 Ex 20:18–21.

The fallen man doesn't want to be close to God, because there are things in his life he doesn't want to see. When we get close to the light of God, we begin to see these things. Jesus told the Pharisees that if they truly were ignorant of their sin, they would have a legitimate excuse; but because they said their eyes were open, their guilt remained.[63]

During their time in the desert, the children of Israel frequently complained about Moses. They were ready to get a new leader, but when it came to meeting with God themselves, they didn't want that responsibility, so they told Moses to go for them as their intermediary.

We can identify with the fear and awe that the children of Israel must have felt in God's presence. We should be careful and honor the presence of God. In fact, Moses said, "the fear of God will be with you to keep you from sinning." But there is another fear that unconfessed sin brings, and that is the fear of punishment. *We only fear punishment if we are not forgiven.* Our guilt remains only when we choose not to confess our sins, ask for mercy, and repent. Jesus said that those who do good deeds come to the light, but those who do evil deeds love darkness. John said it another way:

> There is no fear in love. But perfect love drives out fear, because fear has to do with punishment. The one who fears is not made perfect in love. We love because he first loved us.[64]

REJECTING GOD'S OFFER LEADS TO IDOLATRY.

Rejecting this personal relationship with God and establishing an earthly intermediary is the essence of idolatry. We cannot control the creator of the universe, but we can fashion "gods" of our own that speak only what we want to hear. They are less frightening.

While Moses was on the mountain for forty days, the children of Israel asked Aaron to "make us gods that can go before us." Aaron made

---

63 Jn 9:41.
64 1 Jn 4:18–19.

a golden calf that they could worship instead of God. Aaron was a priest they could control. Because this golden calf represented one of the gods of Egypt, it was a direct slap in the face of God.

> *Then they said, "These are your gods, Israel, who brought you up out of Egypt."*[65]

It's always easier to find a new leader who will give you the answer you want rather than to be responsible for the decision yourself. This is cowardly and dishonest.

There is an unhealthy relationship (in today's terminology, a *codependence*) between those who shirk personal responsibility and those who seek power over others. There will always be takers for those who want to give up personal responsibility. The price is personal freedom.

It is in the fallen nature of man to give up personal freedom in order to escape personal responsibility—especially if man can blame someone else for the results. Adam blamed Eve for his sin, Eve blamed the serpent, and Aaron blamed the people of Israel for the golden calf.

Many "Christians" are like the children of Israel. They look for an Aaron, choosing to appoint an intermediary that God never intended rather than being responsible for their own relationship with God. Most times, it is a Pastor or priest. Sadly, there are men who gladly take God's place.

It didn't work that way at Mount Sinai, and it still won't work today. God was so incensed at Israel's idolatry that he threatened to annihilate the entire nation and raise up a new nation by Moses. However, Moses intervened on their behalf and asked God to have his name blotted out of the Book of Life if God would forgive Israel's sin with the golden calf.[66] But the Lord replied to Moses, "Whoever has sinned against me I will blot out of my book." Nevertheless, God listened to Moses's appeal

---

65 Ex 32:4; emphasis added.

66 The Apostle Paul made a similar statement on behalf of his fellow Jews.

and relented of his plan to destroy Israel. However, he did punish the people with a plague.[67]

There is no good word from the priest or Pastor that will sway God. Each man will stand on his own before God.

WHY DO MEN CHOOSE TO ESTABLISH THEIR OWN MEDIATORS?

The men of Israel chose to appoint Moses as their mediator rather than hear from God themselves. God's intent was to speak directly to the people of Israel to appoint them as priests to a world that did not know him. Instead, the people wanted priests for themselves so they wouldn't have to speak with God.

If you can choose your own priest, you can also fire him. That's why the Pastor can be revered as a man of God yet later blamed for all the troubles of the church and fired. This obscures and deflects the personal responsibility of the people and the men who should be sharing the leadership responsibility and duties.

If the children of Israel had a relationship with God like Moses did, they would be walking and talking with him daily. If the church people of America had a daily walk and talk with God, this nation would have already repented. The reason it hasn't is because God's people are not meeting with him and doing the works he has prepared for them. This distance from God allows us to coexist with our sin. Having a "professional" Pastor or a hired "priest" further enables us to live a noncommittal life.

How was Moses able to stand before God? He was a son of Adam, born into sin. Why did he give up his position of power and wealth in Pharaoh's court to identify with God's people, Israel?

Moses obviously knew God as a God of mercy and was willing to risk his life by trusting him. Because of their sin, the children of Israel could not bear to hear God's voice or be too close to his presence. They

---

67 Ex 32.

understood the God of judgment and power but not the God of mercy and forgiveness; therefore, they really didn't know God.

PRIESTS ARE NEEDED FOR THOSE WHO HAVE NO DIRECT RELATIONSHIP WITH GOD.

In Exodus 19, Israel refused God's offer to be his "treasured possession...a kingdom of priests and a holy nation." He was offering them the closeness of relationship like he had with Moses: the opportunity to speak to and hear from him directly. Because they rejected God's offer, He instituted the Aaronic priesthood that only allowed them to go through a human priest offering animal sacrifices. When Jesus came, God offered this closeness again to Israel, but only a remnant received him. Later, Jesus sent his disciples as ambassadors to the non-Jewish world, offering this same relationship.

Peter uses the same imagery for God's relationship with his church as Moses did with God's offer to the nation of Israel in the desert. Peter says the church "is being built into a spiritual house to be a holy priesthood, offering spiritual sacrifices acceptable to God through Jesus Christ."[68]

How can we offer spiritual sacrifices acceptable to God unless we are priests? Under the Aaronic priesthood, only priests could offer sacrifices acceptable to God. Peter says those who received Jesus have inherited the Father's promise to be his priests.

We speak directly to God, and He speaks directly to us. We do not offer sacrifices for our sins or the sins of others. Our great High Priest, Jesus, has done that. On the cross, He said, "It is finished."

Paul says we are ambassadors of Christ and ministers of reconciliation with God.[69] How can we minister the message of reconciliation to others if we have to rely on another man to do it?

---

68   1 Pt 2:5.
69   2 Cor 5:18–20.

In John chapters 16 and 17, Jesus speaks to his disciples on the night of his betrayal about the unity he and the Father have with the disciples. There is a profound closeness that is unencumbered by a priest. Jesus said we can ask the Father ourselves for whatever we need because the Father loves us and wants us to abide with him, to be so close that we are one with him.

> In that day you will no longer ask me anything. Very truly I tell you, my Father will give you whatever you ask in my name. Until now you have not asked for anything in my name. Ask and you will receive, and your joy will be complete. *In that day you will ask in my name. I am not saying that I will ask the Father on your behalf. No, the Father himself loves you because you have loved me and have believed that I came from God.* I came from the Father and entered the world; now I am leaving the world and going back to the Father.[70]

Therefore, if we are a holy priesthood and we have our great high Priest Jesus, why do we need another man to be our priest? Are we guilty of rejecting God's offer like the Israelites did at Sinai?

The heavenly Father has purchased this relationship for us by giving up his Son, Jesus. There is no need for a priest today, yet we treat our Pastors as priests, much the way the children of Israel appointed Moses to speak to God for them and to tell them what God said.

John said,

> You have an anointing from the Holy One, and all of you know the truth.[71]

> As for you, the anointing you received from him remains in you, and you do not need anyone to teach you.[72]

---

70 Jn 16:23–28; emphasis added.
71 1 Jn 2:20.
72 1 Jn 2:27.

Does this mean we don't need teachers? *No.* The scripture clearly ordains teachers in the Body of Christ. However, if the Holy Spirit dwells within us, we do not need anyone to teach us to "know God." We no longer need an earthly priest. This is what Jeremiah prophesied and the writer of Hebrews confirmed.

> "The time is coming," declares the LORD, "when I will make a new covenant with the house of Israel and with the house of Judah."
>
> "It will not be like the covenant I made with their forefathers when I took them by the hand to lead them out of Egypt, because they broke my covenant, though I was a husband to them," declares the LORD.
>
> "This is the covenant I will make with the house of Israel after that time," declares the LORD. "I will put my law in their minds and write it on their hearts. I will be their God, and they will be my people."
>
> *"No longer will a man teach his neighbor, or a man his brother, saying, 'Know the LORD,'* because they will all know me, from the least of them to the greatest," declares the LORD. "For I will forgive their wickedness and will remember their sins no more."[73]

Don't look to the Pastor or any other human to be your priest.

Once again, it is good to seek guidance from Pastors and wise believers but not to treat them as the oracles of God. You are responsible and accountable for your own spiritual life, and you can hear from God. You should read the scriptures to verify and confirm what you are being taught...even by trusted men and women.[74]

---

73 Jer 31:31–34, Heb 8:9–12, emphasis added.
74 Acts 17:11.

RECAP

1. Fallen man does not want to deal with God directly because of his sin.
2. He seeks a priest to maintain a distance between himself and God.
3. A man can attempt to control God by choosing his own priest. This is the essence of idolatry.
4. We who believe in Jesus have no need of an earthly priest because Jesus has reconciled us to the Father by his sacrifice.
5. Jesus is our one high priest who intercedes for us "always."
6. We are now one with the Father and the Son. There is no more separation.
7. We can once again walk and talk with God like Adam did.

CHAPTER 10

Pastor-King

P riests deal with the relationship between humans and God. Kings deal with the relationship between people and their government.

Just as fallen man wants an intermediary (priest) between himself and God, he also wants someone to take responsibility for ruling his life. From the time of Adam and Eve until today, we want someone else to take the blame for our actions.

In reality, fallen man does not truly want to submit to a ruler. Instead, he wants the ruler to be a convenient excuse for his unwillingness to take personal responsibility.

It is frightening to deal with God directly. It is also scary to take complete responsibility for one's actions. Only when we have an intimate relationship with our merciful Father are we comfortable speaking with him directly and taking responsibility for our own life and its failures. *We cannot have that intimacy unless we are confident that our sins are forgiven.*

In chapter 9, we saw that some Christians want to give up their uninhibited access to our heavenly Father, while others are willing to assume priestly roles that do not exist.

Similarly, some men want to give up their rightful roles in church government and have others tell them what to do. Other men are more than willing to fill that role and extend their governing authority beyond what it should be.

In the Declaration of Independence, our founding fathers stated that men are endowed by their Creator with certain inalienable rights:

"life, liberty, and the pursuit of happiness." This was in direct opposition to the notion that Kings had a God-given right to exercise dominion over their subjects.

Acknowledging a right and possessing it are two vastly different things. Our colonial forefathers paid dearly to win and appropriate those rights in this country. In some ways, their victory could be seen as an affirmation by God that men are created free and as a repudiation of the "divine right of kings."

This concept of self-rule, with God as our King, is also found first in God's relationship with his people, Israel. Later, that same concept extends to Jesus's bride, the church. Whether we are discussing Israel, the United States, or God's church, appropriating that right and freedom comes with a cost; albeit a much lesser cost than abdication and domination require us to pay.

Israel's Example

The children of Israel provide a stark example of how we as individuals seek someone else to take responsibility on our behalf.

God warned Moses that after the Jews entered the Promised Land they would ask for a king so they could be "like other nations." They no longer wanted to be ruled directly by God. The people of Israel asked Samuel to anoint a king, which he did reluctantly.

When God led his people out of Egypt, he intended for them to be a "kingdom of priests" with him as their king. He intended to protect them and lead them. However, he knew that after Israel entered the Promised Land, the people would not want to be governed by him. Just as Israel wanted a priest to speak with God, he knew they would seek a king to rule them so they could be like other nations. Through Moses, God warned the people about desiring a king.

When you enter the land the LORD your God is giving you and have taken possession of it and settled in it, and you say, "Let us set a king over us like all the nations around us," be sure to appoint over you the king the LORD your God chooses.[75]

For God's list of requirements for Israel's kings, see Appendix B— All the King's Horses.

This was not an establishment or ordainment of the earthly throne by God, but a prophecy. God's intent was that Israel *not* "be like other nations." He intended them to walk by faith in *his* ability and willingness to deliver them from their enemies as he promised.

ISRAEL GETS A KING

After Moses died, Joshua took Israel into the Promised Land. They fought the inhabitants and drove them from the land.[76] God did mighty things for them, such as collapsing the walls of Jericho and sending hornets ahead of them.[77]

From the time of Joshua to the time of Samuel, Israel had no king. Whenever Israel was attacked by foreigners, God raised up leaders to rally the tribes and defeat the enemy. These leaders were called judges.[78] Joshua was the first judge and Samuel, the prophet, was the last. This was called the "period of the judges," and it lasted for over three centuries.

During the days of Samuel, the people asked for a king as God had predicted centuries earlier. This was brought about partly because Samuel's sons were corrupt and did not revere God. Understandably, the people did not want them to rule over them after Samuel's death.[79]

They said to him, "You are old, and your sons do not walk in your ways; now appoint a king to lead us, such as all the other

---

75 Dt 17:14–15.
76 Not all the tribes obeyed God's order to take the land allotted to them.
77 Ex 23:28, Dt 7:20, Jo 24:12.
78 2 Sm 7:11. One of the judges was a woman named Deborah.
79 There is much to be said about the effect of parenting by God's leaders.

nations have." But when they said, "Give us a king to lead us," this displeased Samuel; so he prayed to the LORD. And the LORD told him: "Listen to all that the people are saying to you; it is not you they have rejected, but they have rejected me as their king."[80]

Just as in the desert, when the people rejected God's offer of a direct relationship with him, they are now rejecting his direct leadership and protection.

In the desert, when they rejected God's offer of a direct relationship, he gave them the Aaronic priesthood and the law to follow. In Galatians, Paul describes the law as a "guardian" or a "trustee" for children who are heirs. He points out that while they are "children," they are no better than prisoners or slaves, even though they are heirs of the entire estate.[81]

This time the people of Israel rejected a life of faith in God's sovereign protections and leadership in exchange for an earthly king, to lead them and fight their wars. This came with a heavy cost: taxes, military conscription, government confiscation, and a loss of personal freedoms.

God told Samuel that they had been rejecting him since the day he had brought them out of Egypt, and now they were doing it to him. Psalm 81 records God's desire to watch over Israel.

I am the LORD your God, who brought you up out of Egypt. Open wide your mouth and I will fill it.

But my people would not listen to me; Israel would not submit to me. So I gave them over to their stubborn hearts to follow their own devices. If my people would but listen to me, if Israel would follow my ways, how quickly would I subdue their enemies and turn my hand against their foes! Those who hate the LORD would cringe before him, and their punishment

---

80 1 Sm 8:5–7.
81 Gal 3:23–4:7.

would last forever. But you would be fed with the finest of wheat; with honey from the rock I would satisfy you.[82]

God tells Samuel to warn the people about what to expect from their king.

Now listen to them; but warn them solemnly and let them know what the king who will reign over them will do.

Samuel explained to them how the king would tax them, conscript their sons for a standing army, conscript their daughters for the palace, confiscate their lands, and give them to his officials and make them his slaves.

But the people refused to listen to Samuel. "No!" they said. "We want a king over us. Then we will be like all the other nations, with a king to lead us and to go out before us and fight our battles."
When Samuel heard all that the people said, he repeated it before the LORD. The LORD answered, "Listen to them and give them a king."[83]

Up until this time, whenever Israel was attacked, the Lord had raised up men and women like Gideon and Deborah to lead the people and defeat the enemy. Just as the people in the desert told Moses to talk to God for them, these people in the Promised Land were faithless, lazy, and tired of fighting. *They were willing to give up their freedom if someone else would fight for them.*

---

82 Ps 81:10–16.
83 1 Sm 8:9–22.

"When that day comes, you will cry out for relief from the king you have chosen, and the LORD will not answer you in that day."[84]

Israel was no longer willing to walk by faith in God as their King. He knew the desires of these faithless men and gave them their wish. He established an earthly throne over Israel even though it was not his choice.

God gave Israel King Saul, a man who looked just like what they wanted. He was a head taller than all the rest and very handsome. He looked kingly, yet he was an insecure and cowardly tyrant.

THE CHURCH GETS A KING

Like the nation Israel, God wants his church to be different from the Gentiles (i.e., the secular world). Jesus warned the disciples against ruling over each other like the Gentiles do. He established no hierarchy among the disciples and no future church hierarchy. The only structure Paul installed in the new churches was the appointment of elders and deacons.

God's spiritual children—the church—have succumbed to the same desire for a king to rule over them by instituting the "clergy" class. This was not God's plan. It has done disservice to the church by segregating God's family into "clergy" and "laity."

WHO IS KING OF GOD'S CHURCH?

What has all this talk of kings got to do with today's Pastors? The parallels are stark. Christians today rely upon the Pastor and his staff to fight their battles. They give up their rights to teach and provide direction in exchange for the clergy's rule of the church. They place the Pastor in a role of king over the church, a role reserved for Jesus alone.[85] Not only

---

84   1 Sm 8:18.
85   Eph 5:23, Col 1:18.

does the Pastor sit in God's place, but he also prevents the elders from serving in their God-ordained roles.

PASTORS HAVE OVERSTEPPED THEIR BOUNDARIES
The Father did not grant authority to one man to lead *his* family. Jesus is our one and only Savior, high priest, good shepherd, and ruler (king). He is the head of the church.

> For the husband is the head of the wife as *Christ is the head of the church*, his body, of which he is the Savior.[86]
> ...the church submits to Christ...[87]

I have great respect for many Pastors. Many are called by God to his service. Yet even God's men can overstep his boundaries. When they do, I think most do it in ignorance. Many Pastors take on roles and burdens meant to be borne collectively by a group of men (elders). They toil under a yoke and burden that is too heavy for them because it is not their burden. Jesus said his yoke is easy and his burden is light. Not even elders are called to carry out all the duties that some Pastors take on. Deacons, administrators, and men with various other gifts must be appointed.

RESPONSIBILITY VS. AUTHORITY
There is a difference between responsibility and authority. One may be delegated; the other cannot. It is permissible for a person of authority to delegate authority to one under his or her authority. The Centurion recognized this principle when he told Jesus, "I am a man under authority and I have authority."[88]

---

86 Eph 5:23; emphasis added.
87 Eph 5:24.
88 Mt 8:9.

Responsibility, like authority, derives from one's position. However, *the responsibility cannot be delegated*; it resides always with the one authorized to be in that position. Although the Centurion could delegate his authority to one of his captains, he was still responsible to his superiors for the actions of his captain.

God did not intend responsibility for his local church to reside in one Pastor-king; he clearly designed it to reside with the elders of each church.

When men of a church who are qualified to be elders relinquish their rightful role as elders to one Pastor-king, they are attempting to delegate responsibility that belongs to them. For example, when Americans knowingly vote for and elect a godless person into office, whether that office be president or mayor, we are collectively responsible for that elected official's godless acts. We in America and other democracies will be judged for our choice of leaders. Those in China and most other parts of the world will at least have a reasonable defense when they say they had no opportunity to select their leaders. When Jesus returns to rule from Jerusalem, he will separate the goat nations from the sheep.[89] Where will we be?

Similarly, church men who qualify as elders should attempt to oversee God's church collectively, in accordance with the scripture. If this is to be accomplished, it will be done by men who are sensitive to the Holy Spirit, courageous, and qualified. They must discern the Body of Christ and refuse to "split the baby." That does not mean there won't be conflict among the leadership.

Section 8 of this book is titled How Do We Get There? It explores some of the issues that will need to be addressed. However, it will not be accomplished without the Holy Spirit's enlightenment and the commitment to speak the truth in love.

Even so, at first very few churches will attempt this reformation, which is more akin to a revolution. Those that do attempt it in the right manner may still not be successful. I was long-suffering with my brother

---

89 Mt 25

"elders" in attempting to bring elder leadership into our church. Even though we were called elders, we were not. We were merely a sounding board for the Pastor. However, as mentioned elsewhere in this book, I could not "split the baby" by expanding this struggle to the entire congregation. Thus after many years, I resigned as elder.

Seventeen years later I wrote this book.

CHAPTER 11

Church Government Should
Be Local and Limited

❧

J esus did not speak about formal church government, and he did not
establish a leadership hierarchy. He spoke about the heart of leadership rather than its form. He appointed twelve disciples to continue his
ministry and make disciples of all nations.

He told his disciples that the first shall be last and the servant of all
would be the greatest. He told them not to "lord it over" the people, like
the Gentiles do.[90] Paul and Peter repeated this admonition.[91] Jesus told
his disciples not to call anyone Rabbi, father, or instructor. Instead, he
called the disciples brothers. Essentially, they were family.

> But you are not to be called 'Rabbi,' for you have one Teacher,
> and you are all brothers. And do not call anyone on earth 'father,'
> for you have one Father, and he is in heaven. Nor are you to be
> called instructors, for you have one Instructor, the Messiah. The
> greatest among you will be your servant. For those who exalt
> themselves will be humbled, and those who humble themselves
> will be exalted.[92]

---

90 Mt 20:25, Mk 10:42, Lk 22:25.
91 2 Cor 1:24, 1 Pt 5:3.
92 Mt 23:8–12.

The advent of the clergy class transgressed all of the above. Now we have Pastors, priests, bishops, cardinals, dioceses, archdioceses, conferences: a complete religious hierarchy that puts the secular world to shame.

WHAT ABOUT BISHOPS?

The New International Version of the Bible does not translate any Greek word as "bishop." Although the New King James, New Revised Standard, and others translate the Greek word *episkope* as "bishop," the NIV translates this same word as "elder." Therefore, the English words *bishop* and *elder* refer to the same *local* church office (i.e., *episkope*).

Current usage of the term *bishop* in religious hierarchies denotes regional positions above the local level, which are not supported in the New Testament. Therefore, I use the word *elder* instead of bishop, since elder is a local church position and *bishop* implies an unscriptural hierarchy over local churches.

CHURCH OVERSIGHT WAS MEANT TO BE LOCAL AND LIMITED.

At first, Jesus's original disciples (apostles)[93] oversaw the church in Jerusalem. Later, other men, known as "elders" (*presbyteros*), were included in this leadership team. Peter, John, and James were considered the most prominent of the "apostles and elders."[94] Although James was a half brother of Jesus, he was not one of Jesus's original twelve disciples. Sometime after Jesus's resurrection, James was recognized as one of the elders of the church in Jerusalem.[95]

---

93 After Jesus's resurrection, the remaining eleven disciples were called apostles, which means "one sent as a messenger." Just before his ascension, Jesus commissioned them to go make disciples of all nations.

94 Gal 2:9.

95 Acts 21:18.

The apostles and elders in Jerusalem appointed deacons to help administrate so the elders could devote themselves to "prayer and the ministry of the word."[96] In the Gentile churches, Paul appointed elders (*presbyteros, episkope*) and instructed them on the qualifications of deacons. Peter, when addressing local elders in his letters, referred to himself as a "fellow elder" (*sympresbyteros*). John in his second and third epistles referred to himself as "the elder" (*presbyteros*).[97]

Elder and deacon were the only church leadership positions recognized by the Jewish church in Jerusalem and the Gentile churches established by Paul and other apostles. There was no hierarchy governing the various churches. Though Paul went to the apostles and elders in Jerusalem to consult about the issue of circumcision for Gentiles, there was no oversight by the Jerusalem church over the Gentile churches. Even the salutation in the letter written by the leaders of the Jerusalem church to the Gentile churches claimed no higher position than "brothers."

> The apostles and elders, your brothers, to the Gentile believers
> in Antioch, Syria and Cilicia: Greetings:[98]

Paul and the other apostles kept watch over the churches they established, but even that was not an exclusive oversight. Paul acknowledged Apollos's right as an apostle to build upon the foundation Paul had established in the church at Corinth.[99] He even encouraged Apollos to visit other churches he had founded.[100]

It was the primary responsibility and duty of the elders to shepherd (pastor) and oversee the local church.

---

96 Acts 6:3–4.
97 2 Jn 1, 3 Jn 1.
98 Acts 15:23.
99 1 Cor 3:10.
100 1 Cor 16:12, Ti 3:13.

ELDERS ARE THE SHEPHERDS (PASTORS) AND OVERSEERS OF THE LOCAL CHURCH.

Following are the Greek definitions of the prominent terms relating to church leadership.[101]

- **Elder:** *presbyteros* (4565) elder, senior; older, more advanced in years, an elder in respect of age *presbyterion,* (4564) council of elders
- **Overseer:** *episkopos* (2176) overseer, watcher, guardian; episkope (2175) place of leadership, office of overseer; *episkopeo* (2174) verb—to serve as an overseer, to see to, care for; to look at, inspect; to be circumspect, heedful
- **Shepherd, pastor:** *poimen* (4478) noun—one who tends flocks or herds, a shepherd, herdsman, a pastor, superintendent, guardian *poimaino* (4477); verb—to shepherd, rule *poimnion* (4480) flock

The following excerpt from the *Key Word Study Bible* explains the relationship of each of these words. This is in keeping with Peter's use of the terms in 1 Peter 5:1–5.

Presbyteros stresses the dignity and maturity of the individual. It calls attention to the character of the man who should fill the office. *Poimen,* shepherd, emphasizes the work or task of the minister. He is to feed, protect, guide, and nurse the flock. *Episkopos* conveys the idea of authority and points to the ranking position of the official. It also involves his responsibility as one who (along with the other members of the *presbyterion,* council of elders) is accountable to God for the affairs of the church.[102]

---

101 Goodrick-Kohlenberger numbering system.
102 *Hebrew-Greek Key Word Study Bible,* New International Version, Copyright ©1996 by AMG International, Inc., p. 1926.

FALSE TEACHING REGARDING PASTORS

Many people teach that today's Pastor role is the same as the position of elder. The English word *pastor* appears as a noun only once in the New Testament, New International Version.[103] It is translated from the Greek word *poimen,* which is translated in all other instances as "shepherd." Other instances of *poimen* refer to actual sheep herders or to the Lord himself. The verb form *to pastor* is associated with elders.

There are no instances in the New Testament where a single man is referred to as the leader of the church in Jerusalem or any of the Gentile churches established by Paul and the other apostles. There is no basis in scripture for a head Pastor, bishop, priest, or even a chief elder.

In each of Paul's letters to the churches, he addresses either *the church, the saints,* or *the brothers in Christ.* Peter, John, and Jude also address the believers collectively. The only salutation mentioning leaders is to *the saints with the elders and deacons* in Philippi. Although Peter, John, and Paul mention many men and women by name, none is addressed or referred to as "the leader" of their church.

If the Pastor is the equivalent of "the elder," as described in the New Testament, our churches should be led by a *council of pastors* with no single Pastor. That doesn't happen.

Nowhere in the New Testament are pastors (*poimen*) referred to as church leaders. The apostolic teachings of Peter and Paul recognize elders as leaders of the local churches and assign them the collective role of pastoring (*poimaino*) and overseeing (*episkopeo*) the church. There is no mention of a single pastor, priest, overseer, or even a chief elder as the leader of the local church. Neither Paul nor the other writers of the New Testament specify any qualifications for a Pastor (*poimen*), because only the elder role is an office to which a man may "aspire."

Therefore, elders are older, wiser men who function as shepherds (pastors) and overseers (leaders) in each local church.

---

103 Eph 4:11.

PETER'S LETTER TO THE ELDERS IN FIVE EASTERN ROMAN PROVINCES

Peter's letter provides the best example of the relationship between the Greek words *poimen* (shepherd), *presbyteros* (elder), and *espiskope* (overseer). Peter ties all three words into a completely understandable relationship, which is consistent with all the following passages related to elders, shepherds and overseers.

> To the elders (presbyteros) among you, I appeal as a fellow elder (sympresbyteros), a witness of Christ's sufferings and one who also will share in the glory to be revealed: Be shepherds (poimen) of God's flock (poimnion) that is under your care, serving as overseers (episkopeo)—not because you must, but because you are willing, as God wants you to be; not greedy for money, but eager to serve; not lording it over those entrusted to you, but being examples to the flock (poimnion). And when the Chief Shepherd (archipoimen) appears, you will receive the crown of glory that will never fade away.
>
> Likewise, you who are younger, be subject to the elders (presbyteros).[104]

Peter appealed to elders (*presbyteros*) as a fellow elder (*sympresbyteros*) by encouraging them to be shepherds (*poimen*) and serve as "overseers" (*episkope*). Therefore, the mission of the eldership as a group is to pastor (*poimen*) and oversee (*episkope*) the church. Paul says elders who labor hard in preaching and teaching are worthy of double honor.[105] Today, these are considered duties of the Pastor, but they are duties of the council of elders (*presbyterion*).

In verse 1, Peter addresses the older men (*presbyteros*) who have been appointed as leaders. The definition of *presbyteros* is simply "older." Not all older men are leaders of the church, only those who meet the

---

104 1 Pt 5:1–5; emphasis added.
105 1 Tm 5:17.

qualifications and have been appointed. Peter calls himself a fellow elder (*sympresbyteros*). Peter was obviously one of the main leaders of the church in Jerusalem. He did not refer to himself as a fellow *poimen* (pastor or shepherd). He appealed as a church leader (*presbyteros*) to those leaders (*presbyteros*) in other churches.

Next, Peter charges these appointed elders (*presbyteros*) to shepherd or pastor (*poimen*) the flock (*poimnion*) under their care and to serve collectively as overseers (*episkopeo*) by keeping watch over them. Not all elders have the God-given gift to be a pastor as Ephesians 4 describes; yet collectively, the primary duty of the eldership is to shepherd (*poimen*) and oversee (*episkopeo*) the local church.

PAUL'S FINAL ADDRESS TO THE EPHESIAN ELDERS,

> Paul sent to Ephesus for the elders (presbyteros) of the church.
> When they arrived, he said to them:[106]
>
> Keep watch over yourselves and all the flock (poimnion) of which the Holy Spirit has made you overseers (episkopos). Be shepherds (poimaino) of the church of God, which he bought with his own blood.[107]

In this passage, Paul charges the elders (*presbyteros*) with the same two roles as Peter did. *Serve* as shepherds (*poimaino*) and overseers (*episkope*).

PAUL'S INSTRUCTIONS TO TITUS AND TIMOTHY

In Paul's letter to the apostle Titus, he urged him to appoint elders (*presbyteros*) in the churches in Crete. In his letter to the apostle Timothy, he referred to elders as holding the office of overseers (*episkope*). In both

---

106   Acts 20:17–18; emphasis added.
107   Acts 20:28; emphasis added.

letters, he listed the same qualifications, which indicates he was talking about the same office. Those qualifications are discussed in chapter 23.

> To Titus, my true son in our common faith:...The reason I left you in Crete was that you might put in order what was left unfinished and appoint elders (presbyteros) in every town, as I directed you.[108]
>
> Here is a trustworthy saying: If anyone aspires (orego) to the office of overseer (episkope), he is desiring a noble task (ergon).[109]

The passages above show that Peter and Paul referred to elders *(presbyteros)* and overseers *(episkope)* as the leaders of the local churches. In no passage are the apostles told to appoint pastors *(poimen)*.

SHEPHERDS (PASTORS)

There is no church leadership office of *Pastor*, but there is a gift and calling *to pastor*. The gift of pastoring is the ability and motivation to care for people, to mourn and rejoice with them, and to guide them, protect them, and encourage them. A godly pastor need not be a preacher, elder, or the head of a church to achieve his mission, which is to help build the Body of Christ through the use of his pastoral gift.

Ephesians 4:4–8

> There is one body and one Spirit, just as you were called to one hope when you were called; one Lord, one faith, one baptism; one God and Father of all, who is over all and through all and in all.

---

108 Ti 1:4–5; emphasis added.
109 1 Tm 3:1; emphasis added.

But to each one of us grace has been given as Christ apportioned it. This is why it says:

"When he ascended on high, he took many captives and gave gifts to his people."

Ephesians 4:11–13

So Christ himself gave the apostles, the prophets, the evangelists, the pastors (poimen) and teachers, to equip his people for works of service, so that the body of Christ may be built up until we all reach unity in the faith and in the knowledge of the Son of God and become mature, attaining to the whole measure of the fullness of Christ.

Paul notes there is *one* hope, *one* faith, *one* baptism, *one* Lord, and *one* God and Father of us all. "But to each one of us grace has been given as Christ apportioned it." If Paul were talking about grace in the sense of salvation from our sins, it would make no sense. The Greek word for grace is *charis.* In this context it means "gift." Therefore, Christ has given (apportioned) to each of us "grace" gifts. *Apportioned* means we do not each have all the gifts.

Verse 8 says that when Christ ascended, he gave gifts to his people. Verses 11–13 list five important gifts he gave to his people, the church. They are apostles, prophets, evangelists, pastors, and teachers. The heart and ability to pastor *(poimen)* or shepherd the flock is only one such gift. The purpose of these five gifts is to build up the church, so it becomes mature, "attaining to the whole measure of Christ." All five are necessary for the church to achieve maturity.

These gifts reside in men, born with unique abilities and the motivation to use those abilities to achieve God's purpose for the church.

This passage does not address local church leadership. It addresses gifts given to the church to achieve maturity and unity.

Because the word *Pastor* is synonymous today with being the head of a local church, people who have leadership gifts or speaking gifts but no pastoral gifts are often hired as Pastors. Likewise, men *with* pastoral gifts but without leadership gifts or speaking gifts frequently find that there is "no room at the inn." In order for these men to use their pastoral gifts, many leave for other churches or start their own churches, where they can be "The Pastor." Worse yet, many just give up. A true "pastor" who tries to serve in the unscriptural role of "The Pastor" as "the leader of the church" harms himself, his family, and his congregation.

Shepherding or pastoring is only one aspect of equipping the church and bringing it to maturity. The other gifts of apostle, prophet, evangelist, and teacher are indispensable in achieving God's plan to bring the Body of Christ to maturity. We won't explore these roles in this book, because, unlike pastors, they are normally not confused with being church leaders.

GOVERNMENT VERSUS GIFTS

The elder holds *an appointed office* of leadership not based on his gifts but on his qualifications. Although a man who is gifted has influence through the operation of his gift, he is not automatically deemed an elder because of his gifts.

Elders are those who, because of their age, experience, and godly character, have qualified themselves to serve as overseers of God's people. Paul clearly outlined the qualifications for elder in 1 Timothy and Titus. These are discussed in chapter 23.

Paul states that a man with these qualifications may "aspire" to be an elder, and if he does, he aspires to a noble task. One can aspire to an office without having a specific gift. Gifts are given by the Lord himself. This distinguishes the office of elder from men born with the spiritual gift to be apostles, prophets, pastors, etc. We don't call a prophet, evangelist, teacher, or apostle the top leadership position for the church. Why do we call the pastor the chief leader?[110]

> And God has placed in the church first of all apostles, second prophets, third teachers, then miracles, then gifts of healing, of helping, of guidance, and of different kinds of tongues.
>
> Consequently, you are no longer foreigners and strangers, but fellow citizens with God's people and also members of his household, built on the foundation of the apostles and prophets, with Christ Jesus himself as the chief cornerstone.[111]

If any one man on this list should run the church, it should be an *apostle or a prophet*. Note that *pastors are not even mentioned*. This is a list of men and women with gifts for the building up of the church. Paul says the church is built upon the apostles and prophets; not the shepherds *(poimen)*. The passages above and Ephesians chapter 4 refer to gifts, not church offices. Even so, how would you select one prophet or apostle over another? If Paul says that elders should oversee and pastor the church, why did he not require them to be apostles or prophets or any of the other five gifts?

ELDERS AND GIFTS

No one can aspire to become an apostle or prophet, a teacher or pastor. These are apportioned by God as his gifts to the church. Being a church elder or overseer is not a gift, it is an "office" with a task—one that we *can* aspire to. Qualifications include age, good character, and accomplishments. We can attain these qualifications. In fact, the eldership should include men with various gifts, including evangelists, shepherds/

---

110 Some churches do, which is equally erroneous, but the Pastor still runs the church.

111 Eph 2:19–20.

pastors, prophets, teachers, and others such as administrators, which Paul addresses in 1 Corinthians chapter 12.

A man with a pastoral, apostolic, prophetic, evangelical, or teaching gift will always have that gift and motivation. He may use that gift for good or for selfish reasons. His gift is irrevocable. Conversely, an elder is appointed to the office of elder based on his qualifications. If he ceases to be qualified by some action of his own, he can and should be replaced.

Elders serve in shared leadership for a period of time. Being an elder is not automatically a lifelong appointment. Chapter 25 deals with several questions related to elders, such as:

- How are elders appointed?
- How long are appointments?
- How many elders do we need?
- Can an elder be "fired"?

Section 4—The Effects of Pastor Rule

THE PROBLEM WITH ONE MAN having the power that Pastors have can be summed up with Lord Acton's warning that "power corrupts and absolute power corrupts absolutely." This contributes to Pastors' personal failures, which cause the church to suffer. Additionally, the church's failure to arrive at maturity leaves it unprepared for the days ahead.

The role of the eldership has been usurped. Like revisionist historians, many teachers claim that the scriptural role and duties of the elders refer to "the" Pastor. Nowhere in the New Testament is one man given this responsibility, *not one Pastor or one elder.*

There are many men who are qualified to be elders. They have raised their children well and have a call to serve in teaching and leading God's people. However, the "Pastors' Club" will not allow them in. Pastors in a community are like feudal lords with their own realms. Each respects the other's territory, whether he or she agrees with the other Pastor or not. Each expects the same in return. The result is that good men who would be good church elders cannot function as shepherds. For this reason, many simply give up and stop beating their head against the club's door.

Jesus didn't speak much about government. He didn't challenge the authority of the brutal Roman government or even the religious government of the Jews. He did have a lot to say to the Jewish leadership about how they substituted their traditions over the commandments of God. He also chastised the Pharisees and teachers of the law for their love of position, power, and titles and how they prevented others from entering the kingdom of God.

CHAPTER 12

Problems with Pastor Rule

∽⎯⎯❧⎯⎯∽

C hapters 4 and 5 described the poor image Christ's church has in society. Too many times we portray an immature or incomplete picture of Christ. Mature adults and young adults who are not believers see through this and are convinced that this is not what they are looking for. They want more than what is portrayed. Sadly, there *is* infinitely more, but we are not portraying it. How we govern ourselves is a big part of this picture.

There are several detrimental effects of Pastor rule. *Opportunities are squandered* when qualified men are excluded from leadership. The result is that men with different gifts and perspectives are lost to the church; leaving a myopic vision and a much less qualified leadership. The church becomes more susceptible to false teaching.

By setting up an unbiblical single leader, we transgress Jesus's admonition to not exalt one over the other. The clergy is an unscriptural invention of man. It is *disobedience to God's Word*. It concentrates power in the hands of a few that Jesus and his disciples taught against. This concentrated power tends to foster abuse and certainly sends the wrong image of God's family to a world seeking a family. We have only one King.

This Pastor role is *a prescription for failure*. It leads many Pastors into temptation partly because their exalted position leads to pride and in a greater sense because they are not truly accountable to others. In many cases Pastors fall into despair because the task of leading God's people is greater than one man can bear.

Finally, God's church is disunified and weakened by establishing separate kingdoms that are only as strong as the man who is the Pastor. The confrontation between Peter and Paul discussed at the end of this chapter is the type of iron sharpening iron experience that will not occur in a Pastor led church. Because they were submitted to one another, Paul who had the calling to the Gentiles was able to forcefully rebuke Peter and stand his ground against the Judaizers who were seeking to place the Gentiles under bondage to the Jewish law. Peter had been called to the Jews and succumbed to the pressure of the Judaizers because he didn't have the same calling to the Gentiles as Paul had. Together they and the other apostles went to Judea, Samaria, and the uttermost parts of the known world.

QUALIFIED MEN EXCLUDED FROM LEADERSHIP

God has placed in every community men who are qualified to be elders—men whose gifts and talents are wasted because someone is standing in their way. Most Pastors seek these men out for service. However, rather than bowing their neck in tandem under the same yoke of the Master, the Pastor-king asks these men to serve under *his* yoke to fulfill *his* vision and understanding of God. Normally, the Pastor will not seek out men who have the same talents and gifts as he has.

A longtime Pastor friend explained the relationship like this: God gives the vision for a church to one man (the Pastor) and the Lord brings other faithful men to help this Pastor implement his vision. I agree that this is the prevailing mind-set regarding the relationship between the Pastor and other leaders in the church. However, it is not what God intended. It may be great for para-church activities and for other types of organizations, but it is not how God intended *his* church to be led.

As we will see later, men with true leadership qualities should be able to serve under another leader. True leaders have already learned to follow and will be able to do so again when the time arises. However,

Pastors, because of their position, cannot follow, even if they wanted to. The structure won't allow it.

LOSS OF GIFTS

No two people, no matter how godly they are, have the same view and understanding of God.

In Ephesians, Paul says that God's grace has been given *to each one of us* "as Christ apportioned it."[112] Grace can mean many things. We normally think of grace as receiving mercy when we deserved judgment. Paul is obviously not talking about the gift of salvation here, because that is not "apportioned." *All* who call on Jesus and repent have entered into the death and resurrection life of Christ.

The Greek word *charis* translated as "grace" means "free gift." Again, in 1 Corinthians, Paul talks about the different kinds of *gifts* coming from the same Holy Spirit. In this passage the word *charis* is translated as "gifts" (of the Spirit). Later, in Ephesians 4:8 when quoting Psalm 68, Paul says Jesus gave gifts to men upon his ascension. The Greek word translated as gifts in this verse is *doma*. This Greek word emphasizes the nature of the gift as that which has been freely imparted.

Therefore, each one of us has been given spiritual "grace" gifts when we were born again by the Holy Spirit. We did not deserve these; nor choose them anymore than we could design our own hair color, skin color or gender. Paul says that "all these are the work of one and the same Spirit, and *he* gives them to each one, just as *he* determines."[113] Their purpose is for "the common good."[114]

Each one of us has a spiritual gift that we must employ in the church for the good of others. Those gifts become even more valuable when used in shepherding and overseeing the church. Why do we then rely primarily on one man's gift?

---

112 Eph 4:7.
113 1 Cor 12:11; emphasis added.
114 1 Cor 12:7

It is through grace that God gave different gifts to the church in the person of men whose callings are distinct from one another. However, the collective purpose of these gifts is one:

> to equip his people for works of service, so that the body of Christ may be built up until we all reach unity in the faith and in the knowledge of the Son of God and become mature, attaining to the whole measure of the fullness of Christ.[115]

How then, by accepting the gift and vision of only one man, can we reach unity in the faith and the knowledge of Jesus? Why does God give us each a mother and father? The influence, emphasis and manner of a man and a woman are different and those differences are critical for a child to learn what God is like. Remember that He made mankind, male and female, in *his* own image.

INCOMPLETE PERSPECTIVE

How can we become mature and grow into the fullness of Christ when we are only allowed to hear one man's view of God each Sunday?

> The Son is the image of the invisible God, the firstborn over all creation. For in him all things were created: things in heaven and on earth, visible and invisible, whether thrones or powers or rulers or authorities; all things have been created through him and for him. He is before all things, and in him all things hold together.[116]

Jesus is all in all. Likewise his people are vast and varied. Their perspective and understanding is derived from the Spirit that God caused to dwell in them. The Holy Spirit is itself as deep and varied as the Lord

---

115 Eph 4:12–13.
116 Col 1:15–17.

himself. Each human was born with a proclivity to see God in a way that others cannot. Collectively, the church view should be that of the multifaceted Christ. How can we limit our church emphasis to one man's perspective?

Not only do individuals have different views; so do ethnic groups, nations, and races. Can one man represent these views accurately? *No.* He can appreciate and listen but he can neither describe them nor espouse them like the ones who are actually living that view.

Elders provide a much better form of church government, because they are representatives (or should be) of these various perspectives. As representatives of different perspectives they should speak the truth in love to one another in order to arrive at a more mature unity, rather than just give lip service to "diversity." In this way, the church becomes a clearer representation of the true Christ.

This can only happen through mutual trust and love. Jesus said they will know you are my disciples if you love one another. Greater love has no one than this: to lay one's life down for one's friends.[117] What does it mean to *lay one's life down?* It means to yield to one another out of love and respect and to deal with issues—especially serious, important issues within the confines of this love. When this happens, the world will see its Christ. Otherwise, the Pastor will only appeal to some.

Some Pastors try to be all things to all people, and that is not what I am talking about. In my experience, I have tried to explain my vision to a Pastor who had a limited vision of church eldership. He tried to see, but the best he could do was tolerate. Elders must trust the view (the calling, the vision) that other elders are seeing and forge an alliance within the bond of love to help them pursue it. This contributes to Paul's stated purpose of the gifts, which is to "become mature, attaining to the whole measure of the fullness of Christ."

---

117 Jn 15:13.

INABILITY TO REFUTE FALSE DOCTRINE

One qualification of an elder is that he be a student of the Word and be able to "refute false doctrine." One Pastor who has his pet perspective will tend to focus on one aspect of God. That is why it is so important to have a group of committed men to serve as elders. In a family, the husband and wife are equal partners who must arrive at a consensus in raising children. A child needs both a father and a mother. God knew this when he created mankind—male and female—in "his own image."[118]

As noted in the previous section, there are basic doctrines of the Christian faith that must be defended. Jesus, Peter, Paul, Jude, and John all warned the believers about false teachers and "doctrines of demons" that will seek to lead them astray.[119] There should not be a Pastor-elder, chief elder, or any other elevated position above the other elders. Elders should be able to arrive at consensus on matters of doctrine and teaching. This is one of their primary tasks in seeking to "feed the sheep" and "care for the sheep."

UNAUTHORIZED POSITION

Jesus chastised the Pharisees and religious rulers for exalting the traditions of men over the commandments of God. The false church hierarchy and clergy system we have today are inventions of men having no solid basis in scripture. It wouldn't be quite so bad if they were just additional, harmless traditions. But they are not. They *supplant* God's scriptural plan of church leadership and segregate God's people by creating an exalted class, or "clergy."

ABUSE OF AUTHORITY

Lord Acton's observation that "power corrupts and absolute power corrupts absolutely" is never clearer than when applied to a king or any

---

118 Gn 1:27.
119 1 Tm 4:1–2.

other absolute leader or dictator who has no one to answer to. In my social studies class, I was taught that the best form of government was not communism, nor was it democracy. It was rule by a beneficent king. Only our loving heavenly Father is qualified to be this beneficent ruler. Even the best humans fail. Three of Israel's best kings (David, Hezekiah and Josiah) had personal failures that cost the people of Israel greatly. Paul warned the elders in Ephesus to "keep a watch over yourselves." Likewise, we must submit to each other.

Once a man is granted undeserved power and opportunity, he tends to want more. Our Founding Fathers knew this well and formed our government with three branches that provided checks and balances to this unbridled power. Through the Bill of Rights, they provided for a free church, free press, and freedom to dissent. All these, not to mention the freedom to bear arms, are essential to protecting against the abuse of power. The Founding Fathers expected each branch to use its powers to resist encroachment by the other two branches. Similarly, men qualified to be elders should assert their authority to keep watch over the flock by not allowing one man to take over their responsibility.

Unfortunately, revisionists are explaining away our rights and responsibilities as free men in America. Likewise, free men in God's church have delegated their roles of responsibility to a clergy that *God has not ordained.* Like revisionist historians, the role of the eldership has been usurped by Pastors who teach that the Pastor fulfills the duties of the elders. Nowhere in the New Testament is one man given this responsibility.

LACK OF SUBMISSION

One of our elders invited my wife and me to dinner along with our Pastor and his wife. He wanted us to meet his longtime mentor. This was during the time I was encouraging our Pastor and elders to pursue a true eldership model of church leadership. At the meal, the discussion turned to this issue. As I recall, I didn't bring it up. I didn't think it would be polite. At some point, my friend's mentor looked at me and out of the blue asked me why I couldn't submit to our Pastor. I was shocked. Not only did I consider that a presumption on his part, but I also thought it was an inappropriate gathering at which to ask the question. I later found out that my elder friend had wanted him to ask me that question. My answer was simple, "I submit to him all the time. The real question should be, why can't he submit to me?" I explained to him that most leaders are expected to submit to the Pastor, but the Pastor-king is not expected to submit to anyone else's vision.

It's natural to want to discuss this issue in terms of rebellion versus submission. I personally know how to lead, and I know how to follow. The question is, when do you lead and when do you follow? The answer depends on the type of relationship. Like the centurion whom Jesus encountered, we must know our place and time. Sometimes the centurion *took* orders and sometimes he *gave* orders.

> For I myself am a man under authority, with soldiers under me.[120]

The scripture is clear. *All men* must submit to one another out of reverence to Christ. *Children* submit to parents, *wives* to husbands, and *citizens* to their governments. Peter exhorts *the younger* to submit to their elders.

The writer of Hebrews uses a different Greek word, hēgeomai, which is translated as "leaders," but its use indicates that he is talking about church elders.

> Remember your leaders, who spoke the word of God to you. Consider the outcome of their way of life and imitate their faith.
>
> Have confidence in your leaders and submit to their authority, because they keep watch over you as those who must

---

120   Mt 8:9.

give an account. Do this so that their work will be a joy, not a burden, for that would be of no benefit to you.[121]

Equally clear is the absence in scripture of a single Pastor or other leader to whom church members must submit. This Pastor position is a creation of man, not of God. Even if there were a single person to lead God's church, to whom would *he* submit? The answer is no one, unless there was a hierarchy above him. The scripture says nothing about that either.

DIVINE RIGHT OF KINGS

The Divine Right of Kings is a political and religious doctrine of royal absolutism. It asserts that a monarch is subject to no earthly authority, deriving his right to rule directly from the will of God. The king is thus not subject to the will of his people.... The doctrine implies that any attempt to depose the king or to restrict his powers runs contrary to the will of God and may constitute treason.[122]

Does this sound familiar? My friend's mentor obviously believed that the Pastor has the divine right to oversee the church and that all must submit to his leadership. It is not rebellion to argue that neither Jesus nor Paul instituted a Pastor-king as overseer of the local church. The real question is why the Pastor is not submitting to other elders in the church and taking his place with them under the yoke of Christ.

In the immortal words of Mel Brooks, "It's great to be king." As we'll see, it's really not so great for the king, or the church.

---

121 Heb 13:7, 17.
122 "Devine Right of Kings," http://en.wikipedia.org/wiki/Divine_right_of_kings, (accessed 04-02-15).

SUCCESS AND TEMPTATION

You might ask how success is a pitfall. Success is measured in many ways. Generally, we believe a Pastor is successful if he has a harmonious church that is growing. It also doesn't hurt if the church is financially sound and is able to accomplish programs the Pastor has outlined. Yet success tends to bring a certain complacency that leads to violation of basic principles. Put another way, it brings *temptation*. Temptation can come about through success, discouragement, or failure; however, it is particularly destructive when a "successful" Pastor loses focus and yields to temptation. This is less likely to happen when he is striving to arrive at "success."

After David was anointed king of Israel by the prophet Samuel, King Saul tried to kill him. It was about twenty-five years before David took the throne in Jerusalem, and it was even more years before he subdued the enemies of Israel. During this period of time, he depended on God for his very life. He also focused on his integrity with God. Even when he had the chance to kill Saul, he resisted the temptation, saying he could not raise his hand against the king.

David fell into temptation when things were going well. Things were going so well, in fact, that he didn't even go out to battle as he usually did, and that was when he lusted after Bathsheba. Bathsheba's husband was a faithful commander in King David's army. After committing adultery with Bathsheba, David murdered her husband to cover up his sin.

Success brings temptation: money, women, fame, power, and abuse of power—all the things God told Moses to warn Israel's future kings about. (See Appendix B—All the King's Horses.) These are the same temptations that the Pastor-king encounters.

Am I advocating that leadership not be "successful"? Of course not! I am saying that a single man is more vulnerable to success than an eldership of overseers, who not only keep watch over the flock but also over one another

UNAUTHORIZED POSITION

Jesus chastised the Pharisees and religious rulers for exalting the traditions of men over the commandments of God. The false church hierarchy and clergy system we have today are inventions of men having no solid basis in scripture. It wouldn't be quite so bad if they were just additional, harmless traditions. But they are not. They *supplant* God's scriptural plan of church leadership and segregate God's people by creating an exalted class, or "clergy."

Yes, even elders can become complacent with their "success." That's why Paul admonished the elders of Ephesus to "Keep watch over yourselves and all the flock of which the Holy Spirit has made you overseers."[123] If each elder fulfills his role as an overseer or watchman, at least one should raise the alarm when a fellow elder wanders astray.

ADORATION AND BLAME

Pastors receive undue adoration and undue blame from the congregation. Neither is fully justified. This praise and criticism would have less of an impact with an eldership.

Pride comes when someone thinks he or she deserves a position higher than is appropriate for that person. Paul encourages us to rightly evaluate ourselves and not to think more highly of ourselves than we should. Jesus, even though he was God, took on the role of a servant, teaching his disciples to do the same. When they still didn't understand, he told them straight out, he who would be the greatest must be the servant of them all. He also told the parable of the man who sat at one of the best places at the banquet table and was asked to move to a lower position when a more honored guest arrived.[124] How embarrassing.

Embarrassment is one of the costs of pride. Humility is not embarrassing. Satan desired to exalt himself to a place God intended for his son, Jesus. When we desire to occupy a place intended for Jesus, we

---

123 Acts 20:28.
124 Lk 14:9.

operate in the same spirit. I acknowledge that most Pastors do this out of ignorance.

When men choose someone else to do their work, such as pastoring and leading their church, they think they can sit back and blame the Pastor when they don't like something. This is a sin of omission and a sin of commission. They are not accepting their role, and they are criticizing the man they chose to take their responsibilities. Responsibilities cannot be delegated.

CONDEMNATION AND GUILT

When the elders of our church were seeking a new Pastor, we began inquiring of sister churches. In Austin, Texas, we met with the founding elder of a solid Bible-believing church. The only available young man he recommended was one who had committed adultery while he was a Pastor in another city. The elder had counseled this young man and his wife after his adultery was revealed and felt that after a long period of recovery this man might be ready to Pastor again. Although I was leery of this prospect, I was open to it and contacted him. Of course, at the time, I was seeking a pastor who would be a joint elder with us and not one who would fill the traditional Pastor role. Thus the risk would have been mitigated.

What this young man wrote to me confirmed many of the concerns I have about the traditional Pastor role. In his letter, he said that if he ever served again as a Pastor, it would be in a totally different capacity. He would not accept the traditional Pastor role where he made all the important decisions. He also mentioned how he felt this exalted role provided too much opportunity for pride and temptation. This Pastor role, as he saw it, demanded more than what God wanted from one man in leading his church. In essence, he knew he could not carry the same load he had tried to carry before. Although the rest of our elders were concerned with his adultery, I think his lack of support for a traditional Pastor role also played into their desire to look elsewhere.

FATIGUE AND FAILURE

It should be obvious that when one man has all the responsibility, he will have a tremendous burden. Heavy burdens eventually break a man down. Jesus said, "My yoke is easy and my burden is light. Take my yoke upon you." The obvious corollary: if your burden is too heavy, it is not the one Jesus asked you to bear.

Another thing to consider is the yoke. Some interpret this passage to mean that the *other person* yoked with us is Jesus. However, it makes more sense that Jesus would be the team driver and we would be yoked with others who are like-minded. That's why Paul admonishes us not to be "unequally yoked together with unbelievers."[125] Jeremiah used this same metaphor when he told the king of Judah to "Bring your necks under the yoke of the king of Babylon, and serve him and his people, and live."[126] The yoke belongs to the king, and we are yoked with people of like mind in service to the king.

DISSIPATION AND DISCOURAGEMENT

Dissipation means "having one's time and energy wasted by doing things not central to the Lord's calling." Let me give you an example from my hometown. Since my resignation as elder, my family and I have spent time visiting various churches in our area. It amazes me to find out how many new Charismatic churches there are. When our church started in the early '70s, we were the only Charismatic church for miles, and it stayed that way for quite a while. However, now I know of a number of young men who have come to our community to Pastor new Charismatic churches. Some come from larger churches in other cities, and some are homegrown.

Without exception, these young Pastors are hardworking and committed to the call of God. Their wives are also totally involved. Yet their impact in our town is limited—not limited by God, but limited by their

---

125 2 Cor 6:14 KJV.
126 Jer 27:12.

ignorance and unwillingness to unite with each other. Setting aside the possibility that each would rather be king of a small kingdom than a prince in God's kingdom, there's a more innocent answer.

Each feels that God has shown him something (the vision, the call) and given him the ability (grace/gift) to accomplish that vision. He feels (and rightly so) that other Pastors may not have the same passion for his vision. Rather than submit to another Pastor, who will relegate his vision to one of secondary priority, he chooses to go it alone. Therefore, even if he is able to attract others to support him in his vision, he has to build the entire infrastructure required for a community church. This includes church staff, a meeting place, and various programs for child-care, youth, counseling, etc. This added investment in time, personnel, and finances dilutes and, in many cases, outweighs the effectiveness he sought to achieve by going it alone.

I can think of five such young Pastors in our town, and there are more that I haven't visited. Even if each had a regular attendance of two hundred, they would never be as effective as a church of one thousand. A church of one thousand, with five young pastors executing their vision individually and collectively, would dominate our local community. I am not talking about building megachurches. I am talking about bringing about unity to the degree that each elder/pastor need not waste the time, energy, and money needed to reinvent the wheel five times. Think of the collective inefficiency of five church staffs, five children's ministries, five youth groups, and five feeding programs. In reality, each church of two hundred cannot do all of these programs no matter how they try.

Some Pastors say it is impossible to lead a large church with a "committee" of elders. I address this issue in Section 6. I agree it takes a supernatural ability to respect and work with one another as an eldership. Nevertheless, in the first century, the most explosive era of the church, the leadership was an eldership, supported by deacons. As I recall in Acts, Peter preached on the day of Pentecost and three thousand were added to the church that day. Later in Acts, it says that the people devoted themselves to the fellowship and teaching of the apostles, and new believers were added daily. Peter did not lead the apostles exclusively. At times, James appeared to take the lead, as when he gave the answer to Paul concerning the apostles' decision not to require circumcision of the Gentile believers. This was a monumental decision. It appears that the apostles and elders, with the help of the deacons, oversaw a church in Jerusalem of many thousands.

The apostles did not dissipate their power and misrepresent Christ by establishing separate churches in Jerusalem with separate hierarchies. They provided a powerful example of love and unity, fulfilling Jesus's statement that "they will know you are my disciples if you love one another."

LOSS OF STRENGTH AND INEFFECTIVENESS

Each of these five young Pastors, if they survive the stress and fatigue of going it alone, will eventually reach a plateau. Some have already left the ministry since I started this book. My former church is a perfect example. It is now more than forty years old. It has survived all of the above. However, what was once a growing, dynamic church with many leaders and elders has a much lower attendance, led by one Pastor with only one "elder" remaining. It has some impact in the community, but its impact is not what it was when it started in the early '70s and had a viable eldership representing various views.

Other Charismatic churches have followed the same path. They experienced an initial exuberance and growth period. They made limited impact in the community and ultimately settled into a maintenance mode alongside other Pastors in the community, each having his own turf and limited area of influence. The result? Our community is worse off now than it was forty years ago. This is not the fault of one community church. It is because community church leaders have not submitted to each other out of reverence to Christ to confront the challenges of an ever-darkening society. Where is the saltiness? It is buried under the silt of years of turf protection and disunity.

MISSING THE UNITY OF THE FAITH

If today's Pastors are serving in roles that God has not ordained, they will not have true success. How can that be, you ask and point to various "successful" churches. Why did God give apostles, prophets, evangelists, pastors and teachers to the church? He clearly answers that question in Ephesians.

> ...to prepare God's people for works of service, so that the body of Christ may be built up until we all reach unity in the faith and in the knowledge of the Son of God and become mature, attaining to the whole measure of the fullness of Christ.
>
> Then we will no longer be infants, tossed back and forth by the waves, and blown here and there by every wind of teaching and by the cunning and craftiness of men in their deceitful scheming. Instead, speaking the truth in love, we will grow to become in every respect the mature body of him who is the head, that is, Christ. From him the whole body, joined and held together by every supporting ligament, grows and builds itself up in love, as each part does its work.[127]

I question whether Pastor-kings are successful in achieving God's objectives, as outlined by Paul in the passage above. If the members of these churches were performing the works of service Paul mentions, our society would be completely different. Are their members reaching a unity of faith and a maturity that prevents them from being tossed back and forth by every latest fad teaching? We are not seeing the evidence. Our society continues to slide into Godless foolishness, and the salt of the earth is not salty.

I am not saying that God is not working through these Pastor-kings or that the congregants are not believers. I am saying that their effectiveness in fulfilling God's goal for the church is not even close to realizing its potential.

---

127 Eph 4:12–16.

Once again, there is always someone willing to take the role that people offer, even if it is not theirs to give. By virtue of their position, I find it difficult to believe that mega-Pastors are pastors. I enjoy listening to many of them and applaud their skills in preaching and teaching. Some are evangelists, some are teachers, and some are even prophets; but the work of a pastor-shepherd is rarely something that will excite a national television audience. A true pastor's ministry is normally one-on-one behind-the-scenes work, frequently occurring at night or at other inconvenient times that don't fit a television schedule.

In America, we elect our Pastors in much the same way we elect presidents. We elect those who are talented speakers—especially if they are handsome. There is nothing wrong with wanting someone with those qualities, but they are not the qualifications listed by Paul twice in the New Testament for the overseers of God's household.

Unity of the faith does not mean that one view of Christ wins out over the others. Unity does not require us to sign a creed or doctrinal statement, even though sound doctrine is essential to our faith. Our God is awesome, multifaceted, and impossible to put in a box.

Attaining unity of the faith does not mean that the "grace people" no longer emphasize mercy and tolerance or the "holiness" people no longer emphasize personal piety, clean living, and righteous acts. Unity of the faith holds these seemingly opposite beliefs as contrasting views of a multifaceted God. This unity is displayed in the daily workings of the church through people who love and respect one another. This is what I meant when I talked about the one-arm Jesus. We must display the best representation of Christ to our community. It's ugly to see the arm in one part of town and the eye in another.

There are certain basic doctrines, such as the virgin birth, sinfulness of man, judgment of sin, redemption through the blood of Jesus, and eternal life for all who believe. On these we all should agree. There are many other important doctrines that are less clear. In the midst of the Love chapter (1 Corinthians 13), Paul said our knowledge is imperfect and we see through a glass darkly. This is coming from an apostle who was caught up to the third heaven and heard inexpressible things so great that he was given a "thorn in the flesh" to keep him humble.[128] He was called by Jesus personally, a man who in his day had no equal in knowledge of the scriptures and who was eloquent in applying that knowledge. He was visited by angels and the Lord himself multiple times to give him direction and comfort. [129]

If Paul saw things through a dark glass, *how do we achieve unity?* Unity of the faith means that all scriptural beliefs are intertwined like cords of a strong rope to provide the full understanding of the faith. That is what is meant by God's people becoming mature and attaining the whole measure of the fullness of Christ. To attain this, we must tolerate one another, major on the majors and minor on the minors. That is why Paul puts this phrase about "imperfect knowledge" in the middle of the Love chapter and why he positioned the Love chapter in between the chapters on spiritual gifts, which tend to divide us.[130]

INABILITY TO PERSEVERE IN THE FACE OF OPPOSITION

If only one man implements his vision for the local church, it will not appeal to men who have gifts and callings different from those of the Pastor. This is why some churches are driven by evangelism, others by Bible study, and some even call themselves the Relationship Church. I understand the idea of "branding" that helps communicate to others your church's emphasis. However, we are to reflect *the entire Jesus as the Body of Christ,* with no parts left out, until we attain the full measure of Christ. That's why Paul says in Ephesians 4 that God gave us apostles, prophets, teachers, pastors, and evangelists to attain the full measure of Christ and the unity of the faith. How can we attain the full measure if we are limited to one man's perspective? We cannot! That's why we need men with different

---

128   2 Cor 12:1–7.
129   Acts 9:1–5, 22:17–18, 23:11, 27:23–24.
130   1 Cor 12, 13, 14.

gifts and callings in committed leadership who already see and are committed to ministries of Jesus that others may not fully understand. The commitment and trust in another's character is what allows one man to support another's vision and calling even if he doesn't quite "get it."

Take the example of Paul's call (vision) to take the gospel to the Gentiles. Looking back on Jesus's words, we see that he always intended for the good news to be offered to the Gentiles but his disciples never got the message. That's because Jesus's ministry on earth was to the children of Israel. It wasn't until his resurrection that he commissioned the disciples to go into "all the earth, making disciples of every nation."[131]

Paul didn't "get it" either, until he was knocked off his donkey on the road to Damascus. Prior to that experience, he would have never considered that Gentiles could share in the spiritual inheritance of Abraham. God had to take a spiritual two-by-four and knock him off his donkey, blind him for three days, and bring someone he had never met to tell him what was going on. Only then did he begin to get it. Later, God encouraged him in visions and in angelic encounters to persevere. God will confirm his calling to each of us. But don't expect someone else to see it like you do.

After Paul began his ministry to the Gentiles, Jewish believers were adamant that Gentile believers needed to follow the laws of Moses and be circumcised. Paul vigorously opposed this, because by now, he saw clearly that salvation came by grace through faith in Christ, not by works and not by adherence to the Jewish law. For this reason, Paul would not allow his Gentile converts to be circumcised. Even though God prepared the way for ministry to the Gentiles, the Jewish elders in Jerusalem did not immediately embrace it. This was because they did not have the experience and vision that Paul had received directly from God.[132]

(I thank God that I do not have to experience everything that other people experience before I believe them. I have a hard

---

131 Mt 28:19.
132 Acts 9:15, 22:21.

enough time enduring the trials I have been called to walk
through in order to learn important truths. God has taken me
through tough lessons to confirm "my calling." I could never
endure someone else's lessons also.) PL

God gave Peter a vision about the Gentiles while he was staying in
Joppa. This was before Paul appealed to the apostles in Jerusalem concerning the circumcision issue. In this vision, God told Peter not to call anything
unclean that *he* had made clean. He then told Peter to go with the Gentile
servants of Cornelius, a Roman Centurion, who were coming to see him. It
was against Jewish "custom" to enter into a Gentile's house, but because of
the vision, Peter entered the Centurion's house when he arrived.

[Peter] said to them: "You are well aware that it is against our
law for a Jew to associate with a Gentile or visit him. But God has
shown me that I should not call any man impure or unclean."[133]

Peter preached the good news of salvation to all the Gentiles in the
room. While Peter was still speaking, the Holy Spirit fell on these men as
it had on the day of Pentecost when Peter preached and three thousand
were saved.

Then Peter began to speak: "I now realize how true it is that God
does not show favoritism but accepts from every nation the one
who fears him and does what is right."[134]

Peter instructed Cornelius and his entire household to be baptized.
What a glorious and generous revelation of God's salvation to all men.
Later, Jewish believers from Jerusalem came to the Gentiles in
Antioch and began teaching that unless they were circumcised, they

---

133 Acts 10:28; emphasis added
134 Acts 10:34–5.

could not be saved. In the book of Galatians, Paul explained what happened next:

> Before certain men came from James, he (Peter) used to eat with the Gentiles. But when they arrived, he began to draw back and separate himself from the Gentiles because he was afraid of those who belonged to the circumcision group. The other Jews joined him in his hypocrisy, so that by their hypocrisy even Barnabas was led astray.
>
> When I saw that they were not acting in line with the truth of the gospel, I said to Peter in front of them all, "You are a Jew, yet you live like a Gentile and not like a Jew. How is it, then, that you force Gentiles to follow Jewish customs?"[135]

Prior to this encounter in Antioch, Paul had gone to the apostles in Jerusalem to oppose the teaching that Gentiles needed to be circumcised after conversion. Peter, James, and John settled the question of circumcision for the Gentiles. The apostles sent a letter to the brothers in Antioch explaining that they did not need to be circumcised.[136] *Even though Peter signed this letter and had the earlier experience with Cornelius,* he and Barnabas succumbed to the pressure of the Judaizers and did not eat with the Gentile believers when Jewish believers arrived from Jerusalem.

Even though Peter himself baptized Gentiles and signed the letter acknowledging that Gentiles need not follow the Jewish law, he still had a problem fully accepting them. Why? Was he prejudiced? *Why didn't Paul have the same problem?* Paul considered himself a Jew of Jews and, as to the law, a Pharisee. Why wouldn't he have had a more difficult time accepting Gentiles than Peter did?

The difference between Peter and Paul was that *Paul had the "grace" (the gift, the call, the vision) to minister to the Gentiles.* Peter, James, and John

---

135 Gal 2:7–14 NIV 1984; emphasis added.
136 Acts 15:22–31.

recognized that Paul had received that grace from God. *Peter saw a vision, but calling to the Gentiles was not in him at that time.* When Peter was in the presence of those who didn't have grace toward the Gentiles, he tended to revert to his old ways.

This is why it is so important that the church be led by more than one man—men who have received different portions of the grace distributed by Jesus himself. Ephesians says that Jesus ascended into heaven and gave gifts to men.[137] Not every gift was the same. The apostles in Jerusalem acknowledged that they had the grace to minister to the Jews and Paul had the grace to minister to the Gentiles. Weren't they serving the same Jesus? The answer is, obviously, yes. Yet, when the rubber meets the road and your vision is tested, it is only the man who has the grace for the task who will see the job through.

This is why when I brought my vision about elder leadership to our Pastor, he could not support it wholeheartedly. Because he did not "see" the same vision as I did, he didn't have the grace or the desire to carry it out. Since he didn't have this vision of elder leadership, and since he believed his position as Pastor required him to have final responsibility in all important decisions, he could not allow me to pursue this issue.

I explained to him that he did not need to have the vision and grace, because I did. All he needed to do was embrace me like the apostles embraced Paul and support me in the work God had called me to do. But his vision for our church did not include mine—or anyone else's, for that matter. Therefore, I had to leave. There was no way for me to fulfill my grace in *his* church. This is the same reason five young Pastors are laboring in separate fields without the covenant relationship with other leaders like me and our Pastor.

It has been heartbreaking to watch our church over the years reject gifts that God gave to it. There were men with evangelistic ministries, teaching ministries, and prophetic ministries who would have helped bring our church into the mature Christ. Instead, that church presents a weak and incomplete vision of Jesus.

---

137 Eph 4:7–8.

Why can't our five young Pastors join with the older Pastors and other men in our community who are not clergy to present the mature Christ? Is that too much to ask? No, it is exactly what Jesus prayed for in John 15.

Unity of the faith is not one viewpoint of Christ but many views of the multifaceted God whose riches are unsearchable. Different perspectives are not always contradictory or unscriptural. If they come from tested and committed believers, they are likely views of the same God from different vantage points. They complete the portrait of Christ for all to see.

Why must we be satisfied with one man's perspective and calling? This is the very thing the enemy wants. He either wants the church to be split or to have those with different visions form their own churches. Either way, we present a weak, immature Christ with a limited impact in society.

We need a council of elders in each community that can cross denominational lines and present true leadership. Until then, we need a council of elders within the various churches in a community who model this until it can be adopted on a community-wide scale.

The All-Star Analogy

When my son was in Little League, he was selected to the All-Star team and I was asked to coach the team. The coaches in the league made their selections as to which players were qualified to be on the team. My job was to practice with the players and evaluate them until I determined the best position for each. My goal was to field the best team with the best chances of winning while also giving each player the required playing time.

Some kids were good enough to pitch on any team, including the All-Star team. Others were pitchers on their league team but could not pitch on this team. Some were such good hitters that I needed them in the starting lineup even if they weren't good fielders. Pitching and hitting win ballgames.

There was another factor I had to consider before announcing my starting team. Some boys with great talent had serious character flaws. Probably our best pitcher would crack under pressure if the other team started to hit him or someone made an error. He sometimes even started crying. If this happened, I would have to pull him immediately. His concern was always for himself. Other boys were solid as a rock and could keep playing under adversity. They were team players who encouraged the other players even when they were on the bench.

Every team in the league had to have at least one representative on the All-Star team. This meant that some players were not in the same class as others. If we had selected the best nine players in the league, some of these boys obviously wouldn't have made the team. All-star rules also required each player to play at least one and a half innings. This forced me to find a position and time to put them in the game so as not to jeopardize our chance of winning.

How does this relate to church leadership?
First, the body of Christ is similar to our Little League. The league accepts all kids who want to play ball. They all have different skill levels, experience, and attitudes, yet they are all members of the league with the same rights and opportunities.

Second, the coach is like the Good Shepherd. He knows his players like Jesus knows his sheep. The kids know the coach's voice, and it is he they learn to obey.

Third, the All-Star team is like our church leaders (elders), who will help us get to the next level. There is one major exception. There are no reserved spots or quotas for different factions or groups of people within the church. The best qualified men for the job are selected.

Fourth, these men are not selected just for their talent (or gifts). Just like All-Stars, they must have had experience leading their own teams to success. One of the requirements for elder is that he leads his family well and that his children are obedient.

Fifth, success and experience are not enough. Elders, like All-Stars, must not have any glaring character flaws and be committed to the team. They must learn to rely on and support the other team members even when they personally have a "bad game."

Finally, like the All-Star team, the local church needs elders who have talents that are needed at each position. Just as a team needs more than one pitcher, the elders should have more than one man who can effectively teach and preach the Word. Like a ball club, there are times in the game when substitutions are necessary. A player may get hurt and need time to recuperate. When the church is in a tremendous growth period, elders may need men who have gifts of administration and vision. When the church is suffering persecution, it will need elders of tremendous faith, courage, and endurance. At these times, the roster can be expanded, and elders might resign or sit on the bench for a while and cheer on their teammates. Rotating elders is a great way to keep them fresh and to populate the general congregation with men who understand what the eldership is facing.

Nowhere in scripture is the church called to be led by a Pastor. No one man possesses all the qualities that can be found in a group of elders.

For months, our denominational church has been seeking a new Pastor, after the former Pastor resigned to take another job. At a recent meeting where members listed their requirements and expectations, many acknowledged that one person could not possibly meet all of those requirements. Yet no one proposed a structural change. A curious thing has happened, however. The men and women who lead the church have risen to the occasion and worked together in humility with the sole purpose of finding the right man for the job. I sincerely hope they never find him and instead decide to continue to work together.

We have one King, one Priest, and one Good Shepherd (Pastor).

CHAPTER 13

Where Have All the Plumbers Gone?

I was told by one of my Pastor mentors that if I had a vision for church leadership, I should become a Pastor and start my own church. There is no room in the Pastor's Club for men like me, men who want to exercise their gifts of vision and leadership but choose not to split the baby further by starting their own church.

Another Pastor, who is a bit younger than I, claimed that our church leadership was somewhere on a continuum between autocratic Pastor rule and a plurality of elders. He said we were closer to the plurality of elders. I thought differently. On more than one occasion, this Pastor revealed to me who he thought were the elders in our community. He didn't include any of the elders in our church except himself. He told me that he felt a kinship with some of the other Pastors in the community, and collectively they constituted a form of citywide eldership. (For more about this, see chapter 22.)

In both of these personal exchanges I clearly heard that in order for a man to be a true elder, he must become a member of the Pastors' Club. Unfortunately, the Pastors' Club is not supported by scripture. Paul clearly describes the qualifications for elder and how a man must conduct himself and his family if he aspires to serve in that office. According to my former Pastor's definition, even if a man met all the qualifications that Paul told Timothy to look for in an elder, he would still not be considered an elder unless he was a senior Pastor of his own church. What's worse is that Pastors don't have to have the qualities of an elder to oversee the church by themselves.

I applaud the fact that some Pastors in our community work together and acknowledge each other. However, there is a strong element of protectionism in their relationship, much like that in a guild or union.

In chapter 4 I recount a story in which a young Pastor came to our elders for help. In the meeting, I asked him to join his small church with ours so he could continue his real ministry to drug addicts. Both he and our Pastor would not even entertain the thought. In many ways, he reminded me of the rich young ruler whom Jesus told to sell everything and follow him. The young ruler walked away sad that he could not leave his possessions. Similarly, even though this young Pastor had many problems in his church, he had too much invested in keeping the title of Pastor. He could not give up that title to perform his true ministry. We all lost out.

In many ways, Pastors have set up their own kingdoms, much like medieval lords who work together on occasion—when they see a benefit for themselves. Unfortunately, their concern for the Body of Christ stops at the door of the next Pastor's church. Even if they want to, they will not deal with an issue if it challenges the other Pastor's "authority," or should I say *autonomy*, because they don't want theirs challenged. They respect each other's realm and they expect the other Pastors to respect theirs. It is sort of an unwritten code. This is entirely opposite of the way elders should work together and, yes, get in each other's business.

I know a number of excellent men who would gladly have served as elders but could not, or would not, join the Pastor's Club. These are men of impeccable character who possess gifts needed by the church. Their wives are godly examples and together they have raised their children in the nurture and admonition of the Lord. They have control of their finances and personal appetites. They are students of God's Word. Some are accomplished teachers, and all are successful in their secular occupations. Most of all, they have godly wisdom. Why is there no room for these men and their gifts? Some are teachers, some are evangelists, some are prophets, and, yes, even some are shepherds (pastors).

There is truly no room in the inn for many of the men God has called and equipped. I look around the small congregations I visit in my town and wonder: what would they be like if the Pastor with a capital *P* would take the role of pastor with a lowercase *p* along with the other elders in town, and they all were allowed and empowered to minister in the power of their gifts. I am not aware of any Pastors in our town willing to relinquish their title and submit to each other as elders. In some cases, the Pastor should not even be an elder, but that is a discussion for chapter 23.

I personally encountered this when trying to serve as an elder in my former congregation. One of my good friends, who was an excellent Bible teacher, had stood up in a men's meeting years earlier and announced that he was leaving because the only men who were allowed to teach were those who had time to hang around the Pastor's office during the week.

He had all the qualifying characteristics of an elder. He ruled his household well. His children and wife were blessings. He knew his Bible. He was an avid student of the Word who had also studied in Bible college. He was generous and available to help. But he didn't fit the image of the professional minister. He was a computer analyst who went on to achieve much in his profession. We lost a valuable man that night. I knew exactly what he was talking about, because I too worked a full-time job as a CPA. However, even though I was ready to help minister, it seemed that those who didn't have full-time jobs were given greater opportunities.

As I recall, Jesus didn't select one religiously trained or ordained man to be one of the twelve. He chose men who were *everyday folk*. He entrusted the fate and future of *his* church to fishermen,[138] crooked tax collectors,[139] and even government agitators. Of course, he lived with

---

138 Peter, Andrew, James, and John.
139 Matthew.

them for three years. In less time than it takes to earn a bachelor's degree and much less than is required for a doctor of divinity, he taught them the Old Testament scriptures and trained them to follow his example. In response to his call, they left their occupations, their families, and their worldly aspirations. They became available to the Son of God, who changed them forever and they in turn changed the world forever.

I don't know any commercial fishermen in Central Texas, but I did work for a tax collector and was a bit of an agitator in my high school before I became a disciple. I know plumbers, accountants, construction workers, cowboys, and computer programmers whom Jesus has made his disciples. Many of these men are qualified to lead God's church. Their qualifications come from walking in daily fellowship with Jesus through his Holy Spirit. These are men who heeded the call of the Spirit of Christ, not to go to seminary but to lay down their lives and follow Jesus where *he* leads.

Unlike the Pharisees who learned the words of the scriptures, these men learned the *Spirit* behind those words. Just as Jesus explained the scriptures to his twelve disciples, the same Spirit now teaches the plumbers and accountants of today. Where are all the plumbers in church leadership? If Jesus used the common men of his day to change world history, when did he stop using them? Obviously, there is value in obtaining education and advanced degrees, but that is not what qualifies a man for leadership in God's house.

This Pastor system is wrong. It exalts one man to the exclusion of many others. We were allowed to work and support only the vision of the head Pastor. None were allowed to be part of the Club in a mutual relationship of mature leadership and servanthood, as Jesus exhorted his disciples at the Last Supper. Exaltation of the Pastor is not even the issue to these potential elders. But if they are not members of the Club, they will not be able to fully function according to the gifts and calling God has given them.

This is so sad. For this reason, many good men stopped beating their heads against the Club's door. They were too mature and had too much love for God and his people to cause a church split. They took other routes. Some, like me, try to use their gifts without being a Pastor or even an elder. In my case, that was not possible because some of my gifts and the authority that comes with them are considered to be reserved only for the Pastor. So then what? Sadly, many of us gave up trying to offer our gifts of vision, leadership, teaching, preaching, administration, and shepherding (pastoring).

Though I eventually became an elder, I was not able to function as one. Only the Pastor and those to whom he granted the right were able to address the congregation.

CHAPTER 14

Call No Man Father

❦

I believe this is a problem in Protestant churches as well as the Catholic Church. We have elevated the Protestant Pastor and the Catholic Priest to a role reserved for God himself. The current role of Pastor is not found in scripture. Jesus chastised the religious leaders for establishing rules and traditions that transgressed God's commands.

> "They worship me in vain; their teachings are but rules taught by men. You have let go of the commands of God and are holding on to the traditions of men." And he said to them: "You have a fine way of setting aside the commands of God in order to observe your own traditions!"[140]

Clearly, the current role of Pastor is an extrabiblical tradition created by man. In this book, I don't explore the history of its development, since I prefer to focus on the biblical elder model. My guess is that it began sometime after the death of the early apostles.

Here is where I get angry. This is also where Jesus got angry. Before pronouncing seven woes upon the Pharisees and teachers of the law, Jesus told the crowd and his disciples to do what they tell you to do but not to act like them.

---

140   Mk 7:7–9 NIV 1984.

Jesus said,

> "Everything they do is done for men to see...they love the place of honor at banquets and the most important seats in the synagogues, they love to be greeted in the marketplaces and to have men call them 'Rabbi.'
>
> "But you are not to be called 'Rabbi,' for you have only one Master and you are all brothers. And do not call anyone on earth 'father,' for you have one Father, and he is in heaven. Nor are you to be called 'teacher,' for you have one Teacher, the Christ. The greatest among you will be your servant. For whoever exalts himself will be humbled, and whoever humbles himself will be exalted."[141]

Jesus did not

- challenge the oppressive Roman Government or its authority;
- challenge the authority of the Pharisees and the teachers; or
- have much to say about the form of government of the church to come.

Jesus did say something about the nature and motivation of spiritual leaders:

- You have one heavenly Father. Call no man Father.
- Don't lord it over one another like the Gentiles. In God's kingdom, the greatest will be the servant of all.

Jesus addressed the religious leaders of his day. Though he preached that the Kingdom of God was at hand, he also made it clear that his kingdom is not of this earth. He had no words for the oppressive Roman Government, nor did he challenge its authority. He did not even challenge the authority of the Pharisees, but he did accuse them of being

---

141 Mt 23:5–12 NIV 1984.

hypocrites by laying heavy burdens on others and not lifting a hand to help them. He accused them of not entering the kingdom of God and preventing others from entering by being hypocrites.

He accused them of being lovers of position and power, blind guides, murderers of prophets, and lovers of money. He said they love to wear special robes and receive greetings of honor in the market to set themselves apart from their brethren.

Jesus called his disciples together and said,

> "You know that the rulers of the Gentiles lord it over them, and their high officials exercise authority over them. Not so with you. Instead, whoever wants to become great among you must be your servant, and whoever wants to be first must be your slave—just as the Son of Man did not come to be served, but to serve, and to give his life as a ransom for many."[142]

LOVERS OF TITLES

GUILTY!

It's not enough anymore to be called *Pastor* or even *senior Pastor*. We have bishops, even in denominations where there is no established hierarchy. Many churches would not hire a Pastor who didn't have *Dr.* in front of his name.

In one church, I saw a Pastor get down at the altar, and some men draped him with a cape. It may have been some symbol of God's anointing, like when Elisha received Elijah's cloak, but the whole ceremony was creepy and spoke more of Pastor worship than God worship. The icing on the cake was when they referred to his wife as the "first lady" of the church. What does this convey to the church and the unbelieving world about the humility of its leaders? Contrast this with Jesus's statements

---

142   Mt 20:25–28 NIV 1984.

that we should not lead like the Gentiles (secular society) and the greatest among us will be the servant of us all.

LOVERS OF POSITION AND POWER

GUILTY!
Nothing happens without the Pastor's approval. It's not unusual for associate Pastors or the Pastor's wife to become the enforcers. They have positions to protect.

Sometimes these religious fights are worse than those among nonbelievers. That's because we think God is on our side. This is what James addressed in his letter.

> What causes fights and quarrels among you? Don't they come from your desires that battle within you? You desire but do not have, so you kill. You covet but you cannot get what you want, so you quarrel and fight.[143]
>
> God opposes the proud but gives grace to the humble.[144]
>
> Brothers and sisters, do not slander one another. Anyone who speaks against a brother or sister or judges them speaks against the law and judges it. When you judge the law, you are not keeping it, but sitting in judgment on it. There is only one Lawgiver and Judge, the one who is able to save and destroy. But you—who are you to judge your neighbor?[145]

What a horrible testimony and vision of Christ. Don't think for a moment that your community doesn't know of every fight, adultery, and

---

143 Jas 4:1–2 .
144 Jas 4:6 NIV 1984.
145 Jas 4:11–12.

misappropriation of funds by a church member. Satan is always willing to spread the bad news.

SUBSTITUTING TRADITIONS OF MAN FOR GOD'S COMMANDS

GUILTY!

The number one violation of this is the role of Pastor itself. There is nothing more to say. It is a tradition of man borrowed from secular culture.

Section 5—Government versus Gifts

THIS SECTION IS ONE OF the most important and one of the most difficult to understand. It is difficult because we have been taught incorrectly that a single Pastor is the chief governing official and spiritual shepherd of the local church. The New Testament clearly teaches that men meeting qualifications for the "office of elder" are to pastor and oversee the local church.

There is a fundamental difference between a man's God-given gift and an office of church leadership. This is a critical distinction. By definition, gifts are determined by the giver and do not require action on the recipient's part to merit the gift. Gifts are not recalled if a person uses them unworthily. An office is a position to which a person may apply. An officeholder must meet certain qualifications. The office has responsibilities and the authority to carry out specified job duties. An officeholder can and should be removed from office if he or she no longer meets the qualifications for the office. It is a conditional position, not a lifetime appointment.

The New Testament teaches that a man may aspire to the church government office of elder but cannot aspire to receive a particular God-given gift. In the next chapter, the lesson of the "two pots" highlights the distinction between an *office* and a God-given *gift*.

There are many gifts mentioned in the New Testament. Paul mentions five special gifts needed to bring the church into unity and maturity: apostle, prophet, teacher, pastor (shepherd), and evangelist. The *gift to shepherd* is only one of the five, and according to Paul it and the ability to teach are the most important to the local congregation. Just as there is no office of teacher, evangelist, or prophet, there is no *office of Pastor.*

CHAPTER 15

Gift or Government Office

❦

For centuries, Christendom has been taught that God ordained the "Office of Pastor" to function as the chief governing official and spiritual shepherd of the local church. The New Testament mentions no local church-governing office of "Pastor" and no regional hierarchy over the local churches. In fact, the New Testament specifically calls for local church government to be handled by elders and deacons. Collectively, the primary role of elders (plural) is to pastor and oversee the local church as leaders.

God determines and distributes his spiritual gifts to each of us just as he decides our hair color, our height, and other physical characteristics. There are many spiritual gifts. In Ephesians chapter 4, Paul discusses five special spiritual gifts Jesus gave to his bride, the church. They are apostles, prophets, evangelists, pastor-shepherds, and teachers.

These are *men* to whom God has given the special calling and ability to perform specific ministries to build up his church. These men did nothing to acquire these gifts; they were born with the gift and the desire to use it. One of these gifts (the gift of being a pastor) is essential to the local church, but it is not what most people think of as *Pastor*.

A man with a pastor's heart is one who "cares for the sheep" by being there when they need him. He teaches, but he may not be a dynamic preacher. In fact, he may not like the limelight because most of a true pastor's work is done behind the scenes.

God gives gifts to each of us by virtue of our birth. If the recipient misuses his or her gift, God does not take it back. God holds each man and woman accountable for the manner in which they use their gifts.

Unlike gifts, *an officeholder* must qualify himself for the office. Since elders are the overseers of God's church, they must meet certain requirements. The Apostle Paul clearly listed the qualifications for elder, which include experience, a good reputation, and good character. He said that if a man aspires to be an elder, he desires a good task. Men *are not born elders.* They make themselves eligible to become elders by conducting themselves in a manner that qualifies them to *become* elders. Unlike the misuse of gifts, an elder can lose his position if he disqualifies himself. Elders, in addition to being responsible to God, also answer to their fellow elders and the church they lead.

TWO POTS—TWO LESSONS

POT ONE

The *first pot* represents God's choice to make us unique and give us gifts that are fitting with his plan for our lives. In Romans chapter 9, Paul uses the analogy of a pot questioning the potter as to why *he* made him a certain way.

> But who are you, a human being, to talk back to God? "Shall what is formed say to the one who formed it, 'Why did you make me like this?'" Does not the potter have the right to make out of the same lump of clay some pottery for special purposes and some for common use?[146]

Ephesians chapter 2 says that God created us with special gifts for *his* purposes. Long before we were born, God had prepared "good works"

---

146 Rom 9:20–21.

for each of us to do. The gifts that he gave us equip us to perform the works *he* has prepared for us.

> For it is by grace you have been saved, through faith—and this is not from yourselves, it is the gift of God—not by works, so that no one can boast. For we are God's handiwork, created in Christ Jesus to do good works, which God prepared in advance for us to do.[147]

God has assignments for each of us, and we will need the gifts he has placed in us to complete these assignments. Note that Paul says God prepared these good works "in advance." How far in advance? By reading this in context, we see that God ordained each of us to perform specific good works long before we were born. Therefore, it follows that at birth, God gave us the very gifts we need to perform these good works during our lifetime. Paul says we should accept the gifts God gives us—without wishing we had someone else's gift—and use them to do the works *he* has planned for us. This is consistent with the parable of the talents.

POT TWO

In 2 Timothy 2:20–21, Paul speaks of a *second pot*. This time he encourages us (the pot) to "choose" to do something within our power and control. This speaks of making wise choices when using the talents and gifts we have received from God. By doing so, we can qualify to be *instruments for special purposes*, when we would otherwise be *pots for common use*. This is about our character, not our gifts. Paul says we should clean out the inside so we may be "holy" and "useful" to the Master and prepared for any good work. We are not born with good character.

> In a large house there are articles not only of gold and silver, but also of wood and clay; some are for special purposes and some

---

147 Eph 2:8–10.

for common use. Those who *cleanse themselves* from the latter will be instruments for special purposes, made holy, useful to the Master and prepared to do any good work.[148]

What better illustration can we find than this? God is truly extending to us the opportunity to qualify for a better office regardless of our particular innate gifts. Paul concludes the pot analogy with the following passage:

Flee the evil desires of youth and pursue righteousness, faith, love and peace, along with those who call on the Lord out of a pure heart. Don't have anything to do with foolish and stupid arguments, because you know they produce quarrels. And the Lord's servant must not be quarrelsome but must be kind to everyone, able to teach, not resentful. Opponents must be gently instructed, in the hope that God will grant them repentance leading them to a knowledge of the truth, and that they will come to their senses and escape from the trap of the devil, who has taken them captive to do his will.[149]

Notice that the qualities Paul lists for "the Lord's servant" align closely with the requirements for being an elder. Paul says that becoming an elder is a *noble task to seek.* Therefore, we must purify ourselves for this duty and purge ourselves from the filth within, so that we may perform the honorable works of God.

THERE IS NO CHURCH GOVERNMENT OFFICE OF PASTOR.

The collective role and responsibilities of elders have mistakenly been reassigned to the "office" of Pastor. The Pastor role is unworkable, mainly because it is not what God intended. Practically speaking, it places

---

148 2 Tm 2:20–21; emphasis added.
149 2 Tm 2:22–26.

unauthorized power and unreasonable expectations on one man, resulting in undesirable consequences.

In the New Testament, there is no church government position called *Pastor.* We have been trained to think of this role as much more than a spiritual shepherd. It conveys all the other attributes discussed in section 3, such as business leader, priest (mediator between God and the laity), and the highest local church government official. This role is not supported in the New Testament.

WE INHERIT A GIFT. WE QUALIFY FOR OFFICE.

Elder and deacon are titles of church government offices to which men with certain qualities may aspire. In Ephesians 4, Paul talks about men who have a spiritual gift and the calling to be an apostle, prophet, evangelist, pastor, or teacher. These men *are* the "gifts" to the church. The reason God gave these men gifts is to bring the church "to maturity and the unity of the faith."[150] However, these men are not church leaders or elders by virtue of their God-given gifts. In this passage, Paul doesn't mention either of the two Greek words for church leader: *presbyteros* (elder) or *episkope* (overseer). That's because Paul isn't discussing church leadership and government in Ephesians 4. He and Peter address elders and church leadership in other letters to the churches.

The *office* of elder is a church government office. Although the purpose of elders collectively is to "pastor" or "shepherd" the Bride of Christ, each one is not necessarily a pastor. Here is the distinction: the eldership collectively is called upon to *pastor* (verb) and oversee the church, but a *pastor* (noun) is a man with a personal gift and call to *be* a shepherd. Even if a man has a gift to pastor, he may not be qualified to serve as an elder.

Ephesians 4 says, when Jesus ascended to heaven he gave *gifts* to "men." He did not give them *offices.* Like a bridegroom gives gifts to his

---

150 These are separate from the manifestation of spiritual gifts described in 1 Corinthians chapter 12.

bride, Jesus presented men with special gifts to his bride, the church. Jesus calls and empowers these men to prepare his bride for the heavenly wedding. Nowhere does Paul describe the *qualifications* of apostles, prophets, evangelists, pastors, and teachers. Likewise, he does not talk about the gifts of elders.

Twice in his letters, Paul describes the qualifications of elders and deacons. Any man who meets these requirements may aspire to serve as elder or deacon.

Only those having the "gift and calling" may *be* an apostle, prophet, evangelist, pastor, or teacher. Paul makes this clear when he says,

"God's gifts and his call are irrevocable."[151]

Paul refers to his *calling* by God to be an apostle to the Gentiles. Paul did not *aspire* to be an apostle, particularly to the Gentiles. He was in the middle of persecuting Christians and would never have considered that God would do anything good for the Gentiles, until God "arrested" him on his way to Damascus and *called* him as an apostle to the Gentiles.

These gifts were appointed by God to be imparted to individuals as part of a man's spiritual birth. They are inherited from the giver of life, not acquired by meeting certain qualifications.

CHURCH GOVERNMENT OFFICES OF ELDER AND DEACON

No man—neither Pastors nor elders—serve as priests. Chapter 9 "Pastor-Priest," clearly dispels the concept of the Pastor as a mediator between God and the people. There is only one mediator, and his name is Jesus.

The role of shepherding and pastoring the church is assigned to the elders. This is why men with gifts to pastor and teach should be well represented in the eldership.

Since the eldership is also charged with *overseeing or ruling the church*, some elders will have gifts of administration. Elders are charged with

---

151 Rom 11:29.

appointing deacons to help administer church affairs, including business affairs. More importantly, all elders should be men of high moral character and wisdom. They should have experience ruling their own households well so they can be entrusted with the responsibility to rule God's house well.

Other elders have gifts that are more focused on the "work" of the ministry outside the church, such as evangelism, apostleship (church planting), preaching, and prophetic ministries.

Therefore, elders *pastor the people, administrate church affairs, and direct ministries to the outside world.* That is why elders should be men of character and experience. They have different gifts, because the role of the eldership is very broad—much too broad for one man. There is no office of Pastor because God never intended all this responsibility and power to be in one man's hands.

QUALIFICATIONS TO BE AN ELDER

In 1 Timothy 3:1–13 and Titus 1:6–9, Paul lists the qualifications of elders and instructs Titus "to put in order what was left unfinished and appoint elders in every town, as I directed you." Paul relied on Timothy and Titus as trusted coworkers to implement the appointment of elders as Paul and the apostle, Barnabas, had done in other churches.[152] See chapter 23 for a more detailed discussion of qualifications to be an elder.

All elders should possess the following qualities:

1. be blameless, respectable, and above reproach
2. have a good reputation with outsiders
3. be the husband of one wife
4. be temperate; not quick-tempered; not quarrelsome
5. be self-controlled; not addicted to alcohol (or drugs); not greedy
6. be hospitable
7. be gentle, not violent

---

152 Acts 14:23.

8. hold firmly to the gospel and the scriptures
9. be able to teach sound doctrine
10. be able to refute false doctrine
11. manage his own family well: his children should be obedient believers, not wild and disobedient, and his wife should be a woman worthy of respect
12. be a lover of good; be holy and upright

Additionally, an elder must not be a recent convert. Otherwise, he may become conceited and prideful. The term *elder (presbyteros)* by definition means an older man, presumably with wisdom, stature, and a proven track record.

GOVERNMENT OFFICES ARE NOT FOR LIFE

Here is a trustworthy saying: Whoever aspires to be an overseer desires a noble task.[153]

Being an overseer *(episkope)* is a position of responsibility, not a gift. A man must meet certain qualifications to be a good overseer. It is a position to which one can aspire. Apostles, prophets, evangelists, pastors, and teachers are men who are born with special abilities and callings that God gives as "gifts" to the church.[154] Men possessing these gifts are not automatically qualified to lead God's household as elders.

In 1 Timothy 3:1–13 and Titus 1:6–9 Paul speaks about the specific qualifications of elders and deacons. He tells Timothy that the man who sets his heart on being an overseer (elder) desires a noble "task." The word *elder* in 1 Timothy is *episkope,* literally the "office of an overseer."

---

153   1 Tm 3:1.

154   These are separate from the manifestation of spiritual gifts described in 1 Corinthians chapter 12.

The word *task* is *ergon*, to work, toil (as an effort or occupation). Paul is pointing out that an elder occupies a church leadership position to which men who meet the qualifications may literally apply. Oh, and by the way, it is not like serving on a board of directors. It's a hands-on job with lots of work (*ergon*) to perform.

Paul tells Titus to put in order what was left unfinished and "appoint" elders. The word for elder here is *presbyteros*, which means elderly, older, a senior. Therefore, the office of elder should be filled by an older and hopefully wiser man. This man should have already proven he knows how to run God's house, because he successfully ran his own house and raised his children.

In Timothy and in Titus the qualifications Paul lists are the same. He is talking about the same office.

GIFTS ARE FOR LIFE

...for God's gifts and his call are irrevocable.[155]

God does not "recall" or take back his gifts when we misuse them or fail to use them at all. He gives gifts to all men, whether they love or disobey him. How a man or woman uses a gift is his or her own responsibility. As in the parable of the talents, the Master will call each of us to give an account of the gifts that He has given us.

Qualifications for a position of responsibility are not "given," they are acquired. A person who fails to qualify for a position should not be appointed. Similarly, if a person disqualifies himself while in the position, he should be removed.

Therefore, a man who has a gift and calling from God to pastor is not qualified to lead God's church as an overseer if he has not attained the qualifications of elder or has disqualified himself. Here I am talking about a man who is a true pastor or shepherd to people; not one

---

155 Rom 11:29.

who holds a title of Pastor. There are true pastors who have "fallen" into various temptations or who have raised profligate children or otherwise disqualified themselves. In these cases, the man with a calling and a gift to pastor people has failed to qualify as a church leader (elder). This is based on the requirements for an elder to be morally upright and to manage his household well. They did not lose their "gift" or ability to pastor, but they did forfeit the opportunity to lead God's church as an elder (overseer).

Failure to qualify as a public leader of a local church does not mean that a person no longer has a duty or an opportunity to minister to others. He is still a husband, father, and representative of Christ. It means that he has not qualified himself for a position that requires a high standard of trust and integrity in the sight of God's people and the community. That's why James said, let not many of you be teachers, for "we who teach will be judged more strictly."[156]

GOD APPORTIONS OUR GIFTS AND CALLING ACCORDING TO HIS WILL.

> But to each one of us grace has been given as Christ apportioned it….When he ascended on high, he took many captives and gave gifts to his people.[157]

This passage says "each one of us" has been given grace "as Christ apportioned it." This means that Christ has given each one of us gifts as he has determined. The grace here is not talking about his sacrifice for our sins. That grace is not apportioned. It takes away all the sins of each person who believes and confesses his or her sins.

---

156 Jas 3:1.
157 Eph 4:7–8.

FIVE SPECIAL GIFTS TO THE CHURCH

> So Christ himself gave the apostles, the prophets, the evangelists,
> the pastors and teachers, to equip his people for works of service,
> so that the body of Christ may be built up until we all reach
> unity in the faith and in the knowledge of the Son of God and
> become mature, attaining to the whole measure of the fullness
> of Christ.[158]

God sent gifts to each one of us by the Holy Spirit, but he sent five
specific gifts to guide and prepare his body, the church. The purpose
of these gifts is to bring his bride to maturity, unity of the faith, and the
fullness of Christ.

Paul does not discuss *qualifications* for any of these gifts. Notice that
each of these gifts is a person. Nowhere is a man encouraged to aspire
to the position of prophet or apostle or pastor (shepherd), because there
are no such positions. They are gifts that God has caused to dwell within
certain individuals.

Though an evangelist may aspire to be an elder, he cannot aspire to
function as an apostle or teacher if he doesn't have that gift and calling.
This is not to say that God cannot give a man or a woman a primary and
a secondary gift such as Paul had. He was primarily an apostle, but he
obviously was a teacher as well.[159]

ELDERS ARE MADE, NOT BORN.

> The things that mark an apostle—signs, wonders and miracles—
> were done among you with great perseverance.[160]

---

158   Eph 4:11–13.
159   2 Tm 1:11.
160   2 Cor 12:12 NIV 1984.

Contrast the signs that Paul gave for recognizing an apostle with those given for an elder in 1 Timothy and Titus. The apostle seems to have the ability to work miraculous events to break down barriers to the establishment of God's kingdom in hostile areas. The qualities of an elder are those of experience, character, and wisdom.

Paul's instruction to Titus was to "appoint" elders in each church. This was accomplished through an apostolic evaluation of the men in each church, according to the criteria Paul enumerated for elders. Those qualifications say nothing about signs, wonders, and miracles. They address age, ability to teach, success in managing their households, and personal character.

> Paul, an apostle—sent not from men nor by man, but by Jesus Christ and God the Father, who raised him from the dead—[161]

Paul never spoke of being "appointed" or "ordained" by any man as an apostle. Prophets, evangelists, teachers, and pastor-shepherds are born, not appointed. God himself ordains them by giving them the gift and calling them. The gifts and calling they receive at birth confirm their ordination.

The local church may "recognize" and "accept" the gift that God has given these men but it doesn't "ordain" or "convey" the gift. Compare that with the fact that elders were ordained or appointed according to how they conducted their personal lives.

Does this mean that an apostle or an evangelist cannot be an elder? No, it does not. I also think a prophet may serve as an elder if he is qualified. He will provide direction, balance, and clarity to an eldership that needs a good prodding from time to time when they start to stray from the course.

Shepherds (pastors) and teachers should probably fill most of the local eldership positions. This is because the overall role of the council of elders (*presbyterion*) is to shepherd and pastor people. This requires

---

161   Gal 1:1 NIV 1984.

elders to be close to home and available in the community. Apostles and evangelists are usually looking to other fields. However, it is possible that an apostle on an extended return to his home church could serve as elder just as an evangelist who works in the community could.

Paul did not consider himself an elder in any of the churches he founded for two main reasons. First, he did not want to slight any of his "children" in the Lord by serving as elder in only one of their churches. Second, he was not around long enough in any of the churches to devote all of his attention to one church.

I personally know an apostle who was also an elder in his church; however, eventually this did not work because he was out of the country much of the time. An elder must be available in order to help "shepherd" the local church.

> The elders who direct the affairs of the church well are worthy
> of double honor, especially those whose work is preaching and
> teaching.[162]

It is a good thing to have pastors and teachers on the council of elders. I would even go so far as to say that most elders *should be* pastors or teachers. Of course, there will need to be other men with gifts of wisdom and administration to help "oversee" the church. Oversight speaks more to the need to be watchful and make wise, judicious decisions in times of controversy.

WHY PAUL NEVER CALLED HIMSELF AN ELDER

Paul repeatedly referred to himself as an apostle "by the will of God."[163] If it was by the will of God that he was appointed, then it wasn't something he sought or had to qualify for.

---

162 1 Tm 5:17.
163 Rom 1:1, 1 Cor 1:1, 2 Cor 1:1, Gal 1:1, Eph 1:1, Col 1:1, 1 Tm 1:1, 2 Tm 1:1.

Prior to his conversion, Paul was a rising star in Jewish religious circles. He was a student of the respected Pharisee Gamaliel, and he operated under direct orders of the chief priests. However, he was persecuting God's people until God knocked him off his donkey and blinded him on his way to Damascus.

The Lord sent Ananias to show him how much he would suffer for the sake of presenting the gospel to the Gentiles. Not all "callings" are so dramatic, but the point is; *it is God's call.*

> But the Lord said to Ananias, "Go! This man is my chosen instrument to proclaim my name to the Gentiles and their kings and to the people of Israel. I will show him how much he must suffer for my name."[164]

Paul gave up everything and counted it all as garbage for the surpassing greatness of knowing Christ.[165] Because Jesus "called" him, he became a traitor in the eyes of his own people and a threat to the Gentile leaders wherever he preached the gospel.

---

164 Acts 9:15–16.
165 Phil 3:7–8.

CHAPTER 16

The Gifts

❦

THE GIVER OF GIFTS

Every good and perfect gift is from above, coming down from the Father of the heavenly lights, who does not change like shifting shadows.[166]

God is a lavish giver of gifts. The word *grace* means "gift" or "charity."

GOD GIVES GIFTS TO ALL MEN.

He causes his sun to rise on the evil and the good, and sends rain on the righteous and the unrighteous.[167]

GIFTS ARE FOR LIFE.

God's gifts and his call are irrevocable.[168]

---

166 Jas 1:17.
167 Mt 5:45.
168 Rom 11:29.

An irrevocable trust is one in which the grantor cannot change his mind about granting the gift. When God gives gifts to a man or a woman, he allows us to determine how we use them. He does not pull them back when our character is bad. Otherwise, how could we explain the gifts he has given to wicked people?

GOD HOLDS US ACCOUNTABLE FOR THE GIFTS AND TALENTS HE HAS GIVEN US.

> Land that drinks in the rain often falling on it and that produces a crop useful to those for whom it is farmed receives the blessing of God. But land that produces thorns and thistles is worthless and is in danger of being cursed. In the end it will be burned.[169]

To whom much is given, much is required. God expects a return on his investment. Remember also the parable of the talents?[170]

CHRIST APPORTIONS THE GIFTS AS HE DETERMINES

In Romans,[171] Paul talks about various gifts:

- prophecy
- serving
- teaching
- encouragement
- giving
- leadership
- mercy

---

169 Heb 6:7–8.
170 Mt 25:14–30.
171 Rom 12:5–8.

In 1 Corinthians,[172] he lists other "manifestations of the Spirit":

- wisdom
- knowledge
- faith
- healing
- miracles

- prophecy
- discernment of spirits
- speaking in tongues
- interpreting tongues

these are given for the common good…

All these are the work of one and the same Spirit, and he distributes them to each one, just as he determines.[173]

As noted in the passages above, we each receive gifts according to God's will and purpose. Paul repeats this in Ephesians chapter 4:

But to each one of us grace has been given as Christ apportioned it. This is why it says:

"When he ascended on high,
he took many captives
and gave gifts to his people."[174]

SETTING THE STAGE FOR FIVE SPECIAL GIFTS TO THE CHURCH

In Ephesians chapter 4, Paul highlights five special gifts God has given the church to fulfill his purpose. Before discussing these gifts, Paul gives a general admonition as to how we should live our lives and discusses

---

172 1 Cor 12:7–11.
173 1 Cor 12:7, 11.
174 Eph 4:7–8; emphasis added.

God's purpose for the church. He points out that there are many spiritual gifts, but they all originate from the same Holy Spirit.

> As a prisoner for the Lord, then, I urge you to live a life worthy of the calling you have received. Be completely humble and gentle; be patient, bearing with one another in love. Make every effort to keep the unity of the Spirit through the bond of peace.
> There is one body and one Spirit—just as you were called to one hope when you were called—one Lord, one faith, one baptism; one God and Father of all, who is over all and through all and in all.[175]

This is not just a superfluous use of language. It is essential to an understanding of the intent and purpose of the gifts. Ultimately, the gifts are not the focus. The purpose of the gifts is to prepare God's people for his service, bring them into maturity, and cleanse the bride in preparation for the Bridegroom.

First, Paul urges us to lead a life worthy of our calling. This is simply a call to personal integrity. All believers should live a life of integrity, because in many cases we *are* the gospel that most people read. This is even more critical for those who lead and instruct God's people. In fact, this issue of personal responsibility and integrity is the foundation for qualification as an elder.

Second, Paul admonishes us to be completely humble and gentle, to be patient and to bear with one another in love. Why? The answer is to show love for each other and to maintain unity. Love itself is the ultimate goal. In addition, *love has a unifying effect.* As Paul writes in 1 Corinthians 13 (the Love Chapter), love does not insist on its own way and it is never proud. Paul is setting the stage for a discussion of five unique spiritual gifts that could easily create pride and disunity in the church.

---

175 Eph 4:1–6.

FIVE SPECIAL GIFTS TO THE CHURCH (GIFTS OF "BEING")

When Jesus ascended to heaven, he gave *gifts* to "men." Some people call these the "fivefold ministry."

> It was he who gave some to be apostles, some to be prophets, some to be evangelists, and some to be pastors and teachers, to prepare God's people for works of service, so that the body of Christ may be built up until we all reach unity in the faith and in the knowledge of the Son of God and become mature, attaining to the whole measure of the fullness of Christ.[176]

These are gifts of "being." He gave "some to be" prophets, apostles, evangelists, teachers, and pastors. These are God's gifts to the church. They are *men* whom he has called and equipped with one of five specific abilities to prepare God's people. As we saw earlier, these five are not the only spiritual gifts Jesus hands out; however, they are the ones specifically mentioned in connection with building the church up into the full measure of Christ.

Therefore, Ephesians 4 means that men with one of these specific five abilities and motivation *are themselves the gifts that God gave the church.* He has called and empowered them with special "grace gifts" to prepare the bride that Jesus left behind.

Nowhere does Paul describe the qualifications of apostles, prophets, evangelists, pastors, and teachers as he does for elders. Likewise, elders are not mentioned in Ephesians 4 or anywhere else as a gift. They are *office holders.*

A gift is something determined by the will of the giver. It is not a payment for services. The recipient did nothing to earn the gift. An office is different. It is bestowed upon a man who has qualified himself for that office either through education, experience, or other requirements. Likewise, men may aspire to the office of elder if they have attained the

---

176 Eph 4:11–13.

requirements of the office. Unlike elders, a prophet, evangelist, teacher, pastor, and apostle has received a grace gift from God, and that gift can be used for God's purposes or misused.

Paul says in verse 7 that each one of us received grace "as Christ apportioned it." The grace to which Paul refers is not the salvation of our souls, because he does not apportion that. We are not partially saved but completely saved. *So what is being apportioned? The gifts are.*

The important word here is *some*. I believe the Lord gave a gift and a calling to every person when he ascended. However, *"some* were *apportioned* one of the five special gifts "to prepare God's people for works of service, so that the body of Christ may be built up."

Qualifications for the office of church leadership are independent of God-given gifts.

- Not every man has one of these five gifts.
- Not even every elder has one of these five gifts.
- *Conversely, not every man who possesses one of these five gifts is an elder.*

Jesus gave these special five gifts to the church because they are necessary to

- prepare the church for God's service;
- reach unity in the faith and knowledge of the Son of God;
- become mature; and
- attain "the whole measure of the fullness of Christ."[177]

Any one of these goals is impossible to attain in man's natural ability. They are supernatural goals requiring supernatural gifts and a supernatural application. (For more on this subject, see Section 6.)

---

177 Eph 4:13.

Those who say apostles and prophets are no longer needed in the church today are cutting off the two most important of the five gifts to the Bride of Christ, *his* church.[178] Paul said that God's "household" is built upon the foundation of the apostles and prophets.[179] I will not attempt to describe the work of these men in this book, but without them, we will not attain "the whole measure of the fullness of Christ." (See Appendix C—The Apostle.)

A pastor or shepherd's heart is only one of the spiritual gifts given to men as a gift to the church; yet it is central to the Father's goal of unity and fullness. What we normally see in America is that the man who fills the false office of Pastor is supposed to be everything. The congregation expects him to be a good communicator, motivator, public relations expert, etc. Oh yes, and somehow along the way, he is to be a pastor and "feed and watch over the flock." The latter is the primary desire of a man who has the true calling of pastor-shepherd. A true pastor chafes under the weight of the unscriptural role of CEO and wishes he could just pastor (shepherd) God's sheep. Unfortunately, the characteristics of a true *pastor* are usually down the list of qualities that most people want in a *Pastor.*

The *evangelist* who is appointed as Pastor loves to preach salvation and introduce many people to Jesus; but he may not have the time or motivation to make sure that the sheep already "in the fold" are having their needs met. Under his tenure, many people will be attacked by wolves with false doctrine or may drift away because no one takes an interest in their personal lives. These are things an evangelist is not built to provide.

The *teacher* who is appointed as Pastor provides doctrinal clarity and protection from false teachers; but he may or may not be able to shepherd. He would rather stay home and study for his next "sermon," which is more like a lecture delivered by a professor. It may be enlightening

---

178 Lk 11:49, 1 Cor 12:28, Eph 3:5, 2 Pt 3:2, Rv 18:20.
179 Eph 2:20.

but not necessarily inspiring. He definitely won't be the one to lead an evangelistic campaign, but he may write important books.

What about the man who has a great *gift of administration and leadership?* This is not one of the five special gifts mentioned in Ephesians, but it too is a spiritual gift and one that is highly prized in today's CEO-type churches. This man can motivate people to work in Sunday school, raise building funds, and improve the meals on wheels program. But if he is the Pastor, the church becomes little more than another social institution or corporation. By the way, this is where many churches are today. They are efficient, but at what?

Today's "office of Pastor" is frequently filled by men who do not have the gift of shepherding (pastoring). Some are prophets, some are evangelists, and others have other gifts, such as administration. All of these are needed in the body, but unfortunately, men focus on their own gifts when elevated to this false office. They don't—and can't—fully incorporate the other gifts.

Hence the prophet-Pastor starts his own "Church of Prophecy," while the evangelist-Pastor starts the "Church of St. Philip, the Evangelist." Of course, teacher-Pastors like to start Bible churches. Isn't every church supposed be a prophetic, evangelistic, apostolic, Bible church? Isn't this what is meant by Paul when he says that the goal of these five ministry gifts is to bring the church to the full maturity of Christ? But where is the true pastor?

Even if a man with a pastor's heart fills the unbiblical "office of Pastor," he is not always regarded as a good Pastor, because the job description of a Pastor has been redefined. Many times, our churches would rather have as Pastor a dynamic personality or preacher who may actually be an evangelist or even a public relations or fund-raising expert. The real problem is, we don't know what a church is *supposed to look like,* and therefore, we fashion the Pastor into the role of a chief executive officer in a corporation. This is not God's plan.

A true pastor-shepherd's work does not normally get the spotlight. He is the one who visits the sick, comforts the bereaved, and privately counsels the wayward. The nature of his work is private, not public. He is like the family physician. Your secrets are safe with him. Remember the following statement?

> "Then the righteous will answer him, 'Lord, when did we see you hungry and feed you, or thirsty and give you something to drink? When did we see you a stranger and invite you in, or needing clothes and clothe you? When did we see you sick or in prison and go to visit you?'
>
> "The King will reply, 'Truly I tell you, whatever you did for one of the least of these brothers and sisters of mine, you did for me.'"[180]

These should be the deeds of all believers, but they are central to the heart of a pastor. A true pastor hurts for God's people. He will be the first to lift up the downtrodden and have compassion for the sinner. He does all this while not really seeking the spotlight. This is not really true of the men we normally seek as Pastor. Many times true pastors are overlooked because they don't have the gifts that most people want in a Pastor.

True pastors are generally soft-hearted. Prophets are concerned about the direction of the church and the society in which it exists. Evangelists are outward-looking, toward the unsaved. Apostles are looking to start new churches where they are needed and to help stabilize a new leadership structure to nurture them. A local congregation needs each of these men, but not all need to be elders. Apostles and evangelists have hearts "out there" beyond the local church. Prophets may focus outside or within the local church, but pastors (shepherds) and teachers are definitely inward in their motivation.

God's plan is that each of these five ministries be at work as needed within the local church. From time to time, any or all of these gifts could

---

180 Mt 25:37–40.

be represented in the council of elders. What better place is there for apostles, prophets, evangelists, pastors, and teachers to serve? Paul told Timothy, "The elders who direct the affairs of the church well are worthy of double honor, especially those whose work is preaching and teaching."[181] It could well be that God intended teachers and pastors to be heavily represented on the council, but not exclusively and not by one single Pastor.

Is it possible for a pastor (shepherd) *not* to be an elder? The answer is yes, for at least three reasons. First, elders do not serve for life. Therefore, a pastor may have already served and "retired," or "resigned," the position of elder. Second, there may already be enough qualified men serving. Third, he may not be qualified. How can a man be a pastor and not be qualified to be an elder? Simple: God may have given him the gift and ability to pastor, but he has not qualified himself. Worse yet, he may have actually *disqualified* himself to be an elder in a number of ways. Maybe he is adulterous; perhaps his children are out of control. This would disqualify him from the eldership. In chapter 23, we discuss the requirements of the elder's position and the characteristics of the men that fill it.

---

181 1 Tm 5:17.

CHAPTER 17

Gifts Misused

❧

G ifts can be natural or supernatural (spiritual). By definition, they are not acquired or deserved by any merit or work of the recipient. They may be developed and exercised by the wisdom and hard work of the recipient, but they are gifts from the heavenly Father. All people have received gifts from God. How we use them is our responsibility.

Too many Christians make the false assumption that because someone has a gift, he or she is qualified to use it. Many people are led astray by men and women who use their gifts with selfish or rebellious motives. Paul makes this clear when he says, "God's gifts and his call are irrevocable."[182] That means that if a man disqualifies himself from serving as an elder in governing the local fellowship, God does not take away the innate gift he inherited from the Holy Spirit.

The prophet Balaam is one of the clearest examples of a man misusing his spiritual gift. He definitely had a gift of prophecy, but he "prostituted himself" by using his God-given gift to earn money.[183] Balak, the King of Moab, hired Balaam to curse the children of Israel on their way through his country. Balaam tried three times but could not. Even his donkey spoke to him to warn him. Balaam turned to a more insidious plan to entrap the Israelites on their way to the Promised Land. He taught Balak to entice the Israelites to sin by eating food sacrificed to idols and by committing sexual immorality with

---

182 Rom 11:29.
183 Nm 22.

the Moabite women.[184] As a result, God struck the Israelites with a plague. After entering the Promised Land, the Israelites put Balaam to the sword for his divination.[185]

Too often, men are "appointed" to the unscriptural office of "Pastor" without possessing the character and résumé of an elder. Usually this happens because the man has a gift that is desired by the people in the church.

Churches frequently choose Pastors who possess God-given gifts of intelligence or oratory skills. Sometimes they choose the most charming or physically attractive man because they want to look good and present a good image. They are like the children of Israel who wanted to be "like the other nations." They put these "trophy" Pastors on a pedestal from which so many fall and defame the name of Jesus. God's plan was to have a people who were different from the "other nations"—a people who are "set apart" to his service.

So who is at fault: the man who seeks and accepts this position or the people who put him there? The answer is both. Natural and supernatural gifts are a blessing from God to be used to his glory.

God chose Moses, who could not speak well, to lead his people out of Egypt to the Promised Land. He was the most humble man on the face of the earth.[186] God does not always choose the eloquent or the handsome to lead his church. The children of Israel chose Saul, who was tall and handsome, to be their king. He was a disaster. God chose David, the youngest of his brothers, because he had a "heart" after God.

Paul told Timothy to appoint men of character with proven track records who have ruled their own households well. He reasoned that if they couldn't rule their own households, they should not be entrusted with the responsibility of ruling God's house. They must be able to protect the church of God from false teachers and from men with God-given gifts who pervert them for their own purposes.

---

184 Rev 2:14.
185 Jo 13:22.
186 Nm 12:3.

There are supernatural (spiritual) gifts that God has given his church in the form of men "born" with a certain calling and ability. Some of these men may be appointed elders *if* they display the character that Paul prescribes. The Apostle Paul was not an eloquent speaker like Apollos. He had also become a traitor in the eyes of the Jews because he preached the gospel to the Gentiles. Jesus was not physically handsome, and he was hated by the religious hierarchy. Would Paul or Jesus have been selected as Pastor of your church?

FALSE APOSTLES, FALSE PROPHETS, AND FALSE PASTORS

In 2 Corinthians 11, Paul refers to "false apostles, deceitful workers, masquerading as apostles of Christ." Old Testament prophets such as Jeremiah constantly had to refute "false prophets." Some of these false "ministers" are nothing more than charlatans, but others, like Balaam, possess natural and spiritual gifts, which they use to lead God's people astray. Peter also warned about false teachers and prophets who will arise from within the church (i.e., wolves in sheep's clothing).

> But there were also false prophets among the people, just as there will be false teachers among you. They will secretly introduce destructive heresies, even denying the sovereign Lord who bought them—bringing swift destruction on themselves. Many will follow their depraved conduct and will bring the way of truth into disrepute. In their greed these teachers will exploit you with fabricated stories. Their condemnation has long been hanging over them, and their destruction has not been sleeping.[187]
>
> With eyes full of adultery, they never stop sinning; they seduce the unstable; they are experts in greed—an accursed brood! They have left the straight way and wandered off to follow the way of Balaam son of Beor, who loved the wages of wickedness.

---

187 2 Pt 2:1–3.

But he was rebuked for his wrongdoing by a donkey—a beast without speech—who spoke with a man's voice and restrained the prophet's madness.[188]

For they mouth empty, boastful words and, by appealing to the lustful desires of sinful human nature, they entice people who are just escaping from those who live in error. They promise them freedom, while they themselves are slaves of depravity—for a man is a slave to whatever has mastered him.[189]

Jesus predicted that in the end days there would be false prophets and even false messiahs operating in the spiritual realm.

For false messiahs and false prophets will appear and perform great signs and wonders to deceive, if possible, even the elect. See, I have told you ahead of time.[190]

The best way to spot a fake is to be very familiar with the real thing. That's why men of character are selected to run the church of God. Gifts are important, but they can be used to deceive. That is why elders are called to be "watchmen" and oversee the church.

---

188 2 Pt 2:14–16.
189 2 Pt 2:18–19.
190 Mt 24:24–25.

CHAPTER 18

The Office of Elder

꧁꧂

A n office is a position carrying a title, responsibility, duties, and the authority to carry out those duties. Usually we think of government and business officials who hold "office." They may be elected or appointed. Along with an office come specific duties, powers, and responsibilities. These are bestowed by the one who elects or appoints the official.

In a business corporation, the chief executive officer (CEO) is usually hired or "appointed" by the board of directors, who are elected by the shareholders. The CEO and the directors are all corporate officials who are selected by and accountable to those that appointed them.

In political governments, officials may be elected or appointed. In most democracies, people elect individuals to serve in an office until they elect someone else or the official is forced to resign because of term limits. Other government officials are appointed by an elected official or other higher level appointees. Whether elected or appointed, each official has a position with a title and the duties, powers, and responsibilities that accompany that position. Most are required to take an oath of office. Elected officials answer to the electorate. Appointed officials answer to those who appointed them. Neither holds the office nor retains his authority and responsibility after leaving office.

We honor our president even if we did not vote for him and even if he is not an honorable man. This is because the office itself is honorable. We honor the office of the president because it represents the choice made by the people. In essence, we honor one another when we honor the office of president.

In a sense, this same principle applies to the man as the head of his household.[191] God has appointed the husband to hold this office and the wife and children to respect his position out of honor for our heavenly Father, because he is the one who appointed him. Just like elected officials, the most qualified or gifted individual is not always elected. Nevertheless, the husband has the responsibility as the head of his household, whether he accepts it or not. God will hold the man accountable, not his wife. Remember in the Garden of Eden how Adam blamed his wife for his participation in violating God's command. God didn't buy that excuse then, and he doesn't buy it now.

God ordained order in political governments just as he did for the family. By saying, "Give to Caesar what is Caesar's and give to God what is God's," Jesus refused to challenge the corrupt officials of his day.[192] He did remind Pilate that his authority had been given him by God. The implication was that Pilate was not only answerable to Caesar but to God himself.[193]

Paul explained this further in Romans chapter 13. Remember, Paul was writing to believers who were experiencing the worst kind of persecution from a cruel government. How they responded paved the way for the gospel to be spread throughout the known world.

> Let everyone be subject to the governing authorities, for there is no authority except that which God has established. The authorities that exist have been established by God. Consequently, whoever rebels against the authority is rebelling against what God has instituted, and those who do so will bring judgment on themselves. For rulers hold no terror for those who do right, but for those who do wrong. Do you want to be free

---

191 Eph 5:23.
192 Mt 22:21.
193 Jn 19:11.

from fear of the one in authority? Then do what is right and you will be commended. For the one in authority is God's servant for your good. But if you do wrong, be afraid, for rulers do not bear the sword for no reason. They are God's servants, agents of wrath to bring punishment on the wrongdoer. Therefore, it is necessary to submit to the authorities, not only because of possible punishment but also as a matter of conscience.

This is also why you pay taxes, for the authorities are God's servants, who give their full time to governing. Give to everyone what you owe them: If you owe taxes, pay taxes; if revenue, then revenue; if respect, then respect; if honor, then honor.[194]

As with most general rules, there are exceptions. This applies to government rule as well as family rule. When governments say you cannot preach in the name of Jesus, you have a decision to make just like Peter and John did.

Then they (the Sanhedrin) called them in again and commanded them not to speak or teach at all in the name of Jesus. But Peter and John replied, "Which is right in God's eyes: to listen to you, or to him? You be the judges! As for us, we cannot help speaking about what we have seen and heard."[195]

Likewise, a woman has an obligation to protect her children and herself from physical abuse.

With the office comes responsibility for the use of its authority. God will judge Pilate for his decision to torture and execute the Christ. God even gave him a warning through his wife's dream. Likewise, the Sanhedrin will be judged for demanding Jesus's death when Pilate found him innocent three times.[196]

---

194 Rom 13:1–7.
195 Acts 4:18-20 (emphasis added)
196 Lk 23:1–23.

Every believer or nonbeliever who holds a position of responsibility will give account to God, just as every person will give an account for his or her use of God-given gifts.

Have confidence in your leaders and submit to their authority, because they keep watch over you as those who must give an account. Do this so that their work will be a joy, not a burden, for that would be of no benefit to you.[197]

The office of elder and the office of deacon are the only church government offices spoken of in the New Testament. Although the purpose of elders as a collective group is to "pastor or shepherd" the church, that role has been usurped. It has been assigned to "The Pastor," an office not found in the New Testament. Because the primary role of the elders has been reassigned to the Pastor, most people have a difficult time understanding why elders are needed. Without their office and authority, elders appear to be useless and superfluous. In fact, without official recognition and authority they *are* useless for God's purpose of pastoring and governing. Many times, the congregation views them as impediments to the Pastor. I am not aware of many examples in America where God's order for his local church is functioning. (See chapter 21 for one good example.)

If God is interested in the government of our families and our secular societies, how much more does he take an interest in the government of his church: the body and bride of his son Jesus? For a more in-depth discussion of the qualifications and duties of the office of elder read chapters 23 and 24.

---

197 Heb 13:17.

Section 6—A Higher Calling

SOME SAY GOVERNMENT BY A committed group of elders is unnatural and impractical; it can't be done. They say the buck has to stop somewhere, and therefore we need a hierarchy. But as we see in "A Spider's Tale," the Christian walk itself is unnatural. It's supernatural! God has called every Christian to walk by the Spirit (supernatural) and not by the flesh (natural).[198] So why should it be a surprise that he has called men of the church to adopt a leadership structure that will not work in our natural world?

In "There Needs to Be a Wedding," I describe the relationship elders should have with each other. They should be able to demonstrate the Father's love and direction and live in supernatural submission and love toward each other as an example of leadership very different from the natural world.

"Kingston upon Thames, A Good Example," is a story about a church I knew in the early 1970s from my days in England. I was the leader of one of the first Christian rock bands in the United States and Great Britain. This was our church away from home. I don't know how they are now, but the example they gave to us showed me that many of the things I espouse in this book can be and have been done.

---

198 Gal 5:16.

CHAPTER 19

A Spider's Tale

❧

TWO SPIDERS

One day our Pastor told me a story about two spiders he watched at his house. He noticed they were both on the same web. When he returned some time later, he noticed there was only one.

This was during the time I was still an elder. He and I had already discussed many of the issues in this book. He later recounted the story in an elder's meeting. His conclusion was that it is not natural for two leaders to coexist in one realm. One or the other will have to submit or, as in this case, leave the web.

THE NATURAL WORLD
(TO THE VICTOR BELONG THE SPOILS)

I am a hunter. I hunt deer, wild hogs, and, if I get the chance, elk and antelope. During my many years in the field, I have spent hours observing animal behavior. I have also observed the natural order of the animal kingdom. During the mating season, the males fight with each other to establish dominance and the "right" to court the females. The fact that the dominant male gets to pass on his "superior" genes through his harem of does, sows, or cows seems to support the theory known as "survival of the fittest."

This is the natural order of things, and it is no different with human "animals." We have all observed the mating ritual. We have also observed that the strong and the crafty succeed. *Success* in our culture is defined as attaining wealth and power.

One of the natural keys to success is beauty. It is a documented fact that politicians, business leaders, and yes, Pastors, have a leg up on the competition if they are handsome. How many ugly presidents have been elected since the advent of television? John Kennedy defeated Richard Nixon in 1960. It was the first presidential campaign that most Americans followed on TV. The contrasting appearances of the two men during a crucial TV debate clearly favored Kennedy.

Other keys to success are a charming personality and a quick mind. These qualities are bestowed by our Creator from the natural gene pool. I can groom myself well and have cosmetic surgery, but I will never be as handsome as a movie star. I can improve the way I present myself to others, but I will never be as likeable or charming as some of my friends.

Still others achieve success by inheritance. Even though they themselves may not possess the inherent qualities mentioned above, their families are already successful, wealthy, and powerful.

NATURAL, SUBNATURAL, AND SUPERNATURAL

God created Adam and Eve (mankind) in his own image. He gave man a mind and a free will to rise above his natural tendencies, to live a life higher than animals that live according to their natural instincts. Unfortunately, man can also "choose" to operate below his natural instincts and become baser than his animal cousins.

> For although they knew God, they neither glorified him as God nor gave thanks to him, but their thinking became futile and their foolish hearts were darkened.[199]

What mama bear doesn't defend her cubs against all comers, even from the larger males? Yet we hear horrific stories of women who

---

199 Rom 1:21.

abandon or abuse their babies in ways that I won't describe. The scripture says we shouldn't even discuss these horrible acts that have now become scripts for books, movies, and television shows. I focus here on a mother's natural instinct to protect her young because it is so easily understood. Fathers commit equally subnatural acts.

Because all men are created in God's image, we have a mind and a will that is superior to all the animal kingdom. I have heard that the definition of a mind is a brain with a will. With our minds, we can agree with God and live a supernatural life, or we can agree with the god of this world and live a subnatural life by participating in activities that would be *unnatural* to the animal world.

The story of the two spiders is one of natural animal instincts. There is no moral issue here. Animals behave according to their innate instincts. However, man, and especially the regenerated Christian, is expected to live a supernatural life. All humans are made in the image of God, with at least some basic knowledge of God and an internal moral guide.

Paul encourages us by saying, "Since, then, you have been raised with Christ, set your hearts on things above, where Christ is seated at the right hand of God."[200]

Again, Paul tells the Philippians "Finally, brothers and sisters, whatever is true, whatever is noble, whatever is right, whatever is pure, whatever is lovely, whatever is admirable—if anything is excellent or praiseworthy—think about such things."[201] These are calls to lead a supernatural life.

The distinction between a natural and a supernatural life is never clearer than when applying these concepts to leadership. Jesus admonished his followers not to lord it over one another as the Gentiles do.[202] Translation: the Gentiles follow the natural order of leadership, and to the victor belong the spoils. We are called to a higher, supernatural way of leadership. When James and John came to Jesus asking that they be

[200] Col 3:1 NIV 1984.
[201] Phil 4:8
[202] Mt 20:25, Mk 10:42, Lk 22:25, 2 Cor 1:24, 1 Pt 5:3.

granted positions of power and status in the kingdom second only to him, he told them they didn't understand what they were asking.[203]

Jesus explained that in his kingdom, the first will be last and the last will be first. He told the parable of the man who chose the seat of honor at a banquet and was told to move. Paul said we must think of others more highly than ourselves. This is talk that the natural man does not understand. In fact, this attitude is ridiculed in many corporate and political environments. I personally have seen managers regard an attitude of humility and kindness to other employees as a sign of weakness. Although we give it lip service in our churches, we still tend to choose our leaders in a very worldly and natural way (i.e., like the Gentiles do).

IT ISN'T PRACTICAL

This is one of the favorite objections to elder rule. On one of my hunting trips, I discussed this issue of supernatural leadership with a former Pastor as it relates to elders submitting to one another. His response was that this type of leadership is not workable. He said it is unnatural for there not to be a dominant leader, and wherever he has seen it tried, it failed. He recommended that I go and start my own church. I explained that I did not want to start my own church. I wanted to be an elder in a church where its leaders choose a supernatural way of submitting and working together. I wanted to see the local church united in its strengths and talents rather than fragmented and weakened by each leader trying to establish his vision.

Another dynamic of natural leadership is also evident in the animal kingdom. After being run off by the dominant male, weaker males either try to establish their own harem by running off weaker, younger males in other areas, or they become "satellite" bulls. This is not unlike the way the church handles leadership. Some Pastors are considered unsuited to run a megachurch, but they can handle a church of two hundred. Others are not considered capable of being a senior Pastor at

---

203 Mk 10:35–45.

all, so they become an associate Pastor to the senior Pastor. Still others may become like the satellite bulls, picking off stray cows whenever the dominant bull is not watching or is weakened in some manner. *None of these is an example of kingdom leadership.*

A HIGHER CALLING

The natural tendencies of a male are to dominate and control as much as he can, whether it be money, power, fame, or women. Yet God has called men to a higher way.

God calls every Christian to walk by the Spirit [supernatural] and not by the flesh [natural].[204] So why should it be a surprise that he has called men of the church to adopt a leadership structure that will not work in our natural world? An elder-led church is the only scriptural model, but it can only be achieved through supernatural leadership.

With God, all things are possible if we submit to the heavenly Father.[205] Though the model of church leadership presented in this book may appear impractical and even impossible, how is it any different from other aspects of a Christian's life?

During Jesus's days on earth, his followers knew they could not adhere to the legalistic requirements of the Mosaic laws any better than the fanatical Pharisees. The Pharisees considered themselves to be the most righteous of all the Jews because of their compulsive attention to the letter of the law.

In the Sermon on the Mount, Jesus set the bar for moral living much higher than the Jewish law. He set it so high, in fact, that the hearers immediately knew it was impossible for them to attain. Jesus told his followers that if their righteousness did not exceed that of the Pharisees, they would not see the kingdom of God.

---

204 Rom 8:1–4, Gal 5:16, 25 Eph 2:2–3.
205 Mt 19:16–26.

Murder

"You have heard that it was said to the people long ago, 'You shall not murder, and anyone who murders will be subject to judgment.' But I tell you that anyone who is angry with a brother or sister will be subject to judgment. Again, anyone who says to a brother or sister, 'Raca,' is answerable to the court. And anyone who says, 'You fool!' will be in danger of the fire of hell."[206]

Adultery

"You have heard that it was said, 'You shall not commit adultery.' But I tell you that anyone who looks at a woman lustfully has already committed adultery with her in his heart."[207]

Divorce

"It has been said, 'Anyone who divorces his wife must give her a certificate of divorce.' But I tell you that anyone who divorces his wife, except for sexual immorality, makes her the victim of adultery, and anyone who marries a divorced woman commits adultery."[208]

Oaths

"Again, you have heard that it was said to the people long ago, 'Do not break your oath, but fulfill to the Lord the vows you have made.' But I tell you, do not swear an oath at all: either by heaven, for it is God's throne; or by the earth, for it is his footstool; or by Jerusalem, for it is the city of the Great King. And do not swear by your head, for you cannot make even one hair white or black.

---

206 Mt 5:21–22.
207 Mt 5:27–29.
208 Mt 5:31–32.

All you need to say is simply 'Yes' or 'No'; anything beyond this comes from the evil one."[209]

Eye for Eye

"You have heard that it was said, 'Eye for eye, and tooth for tooth.' But I tell you, do not resist an evil person. If anyone slaps you on the right cheek, turn to them the other cheek also. And if anyone wants to sue you and take your shirt, hand over your coat as well. If anyone forces you to go one mile, go with them two miles. Give to the one who asks you, and do not turn away from the one who wants to borrow from you."[210]

Love for Enemies

"You have heard that it was said, 'Love your neighbor and hate your enemy.' But I tell you, love your enemies and pray for those who persecute you, that you may be children of your Father in heaven. He causes his sun to rise on the evil and the good, and sends rain on the righteous and the unrighteous. If you love those who love you, what reward will you get? Are not even the tax collectors doing that? And if you greet only your own people, what are you doing more than others? Do not even pagans do that? Be perfect, therefore, as your heavenly Father is perfect."[211]

"Be perfect?" I have transgressed all of the above. It's impossible for me not to call a fool a fool. It's not "practical" to pray for someone who has stolen from me. It's not "reasonable" to pray for a tyrant who fired me or my wife without giving notice or a reason. It's impossible,

209 Mt 5:33–37.
210 Mt 5:38–42.
211 Mt 5:43–48.

impractical, and unreasonable for the natural man; but with God all things are possible.

But We Have the Mind of Christ[212]

> The Spirit searches all things, even the deep things of God. For who knows a person's thoughts except their own spirit within them? In the same way no one knows the thoughts of God except the Spirit of God. What we have received is not the spirit of the world, but the Spirit who is from God, so that we may understand what God has freely given us. This is what we speak, not in words taught us by human wisdom but in words taught by the Spirit, explaining spiritual realities with Spirit-taught words.
>
> The person without the Spirit does not accept the things that come from the Spirit of God but considers them foolishness, and cannot understand them because they are discerned only through the Spirit. The person with the Spirit makes judgments about all things...[213]

Is it *possible* for a man not to lust in his heart? Is it possible for us to pray for those who despitefully use us, to turn the other cheek, to go the extra mile, to give our cloak as well as our coat? Yes, it is, but it is not "natural." As Paul said, these are spiritual realities, not fables. However, those who think according to the natural way of life consider the *realities* of the supernatural life to be "foolishness."

Can a Christian operate in the natural way and not even attempt the supernatural? Yes, of course. In fact, it is only through the renewing of our minds by the Holy Spirit, which God has caused to dwell within

---

212 1 Cor 2:16.
213 1 Cor 2:11–15.

us that we dare to attempt these works of faith and accomplish supernatural realities. This does not happen overnight. It is something we practice. We overcome one battle after another; just as David killed the lion, then the bear, and then Goliath. Although his foes became increasingly stronger, David's response to each was to stand his ground in faith rather than turn and run.

> Do not conform to the pattern of this world, but be transformed
> by the renewing of your mind.[214]

The old Adam in us won't be able to do this. He sold us into slavery through his sin. Jesus is the new Adam. By the Holy Spirit, Jesus fulfilled the high standard he taught his disciples by living a sinless life. When we accept *his* new life, we too can do greater things in a higher realm. We are not sinless, as he was, but after being born again by the Holy Spirit, we begin to transform and renew our minds. With God's help, I have been able to accomplish some of these spiritual realities that I previously could not.

HOW DOES THIS RELATE TO CHURCH LEADERSHIP?

If Jesus is calling all of us individually to a supernatural, moral life, why shouldn't the Father expect the leaders of his church to submit to one another out of respect for him and his children? Section 7, How Does This Work? provides further explanation. If we believe in the virgin birth, this should be a cinch.

---

214 Rom 12:2.

CHAPTER 20

There Needs to Be a Wedding

❦

Unity and love are evidence to the unbelieving world that what we preach is what we believe. Jesus said they will know you are my disciples if you love one another.[215] Unity is an outgrowth of that love. How much do we love one another if we can't worship together in the same place or work on the same evangelistic outreaches? Why does every little church have to have its own Sunday school, board of directors, Pastor, and church staff? What a waste! This is evidence to the world that we don't really like each other very much. We are sort of like estranged family members. Yes, we have the same parentage, but we don't really enjoy being around each other. Sometimes the feelings are worse. The prophet said of the faithless Jews, "because of you my name is blasphemed in front of the Gentiles."[216]

Admittedly, some Pastors reach out to other Pastors in attempts to unify. They hold pastoral prayer sessions and even work together to hold joint worship services and evangelistic outreaches. In rare cases, as was true with our Pastor, they even exchange pulpits and speak to each other's congregations. However, that is the problem. These are not *their* congregations. No matter how much these Pastors get together and sing "Kumbaya," the fact remains: they still have separate "turfs." We have separate buildings, separate names, separate goals, and separate plans.

I agree that true unity is of the Spirit and is not accomplished by bringing everyone under one roof. However, where there is true unity, there

---

215 Jn 13:35.
216 Rom 2:24.

will be a desire to eliminate boundaries and become one in a way that others can see. Such was the testimony of the early church in Jerusalem.

THE FELLOWSHIP OF THE BELIEVERS

They devoted themselves to the apostles' teaching and to fellowship, to the breaking of bread and to prayer. Everyone was filled with awe at the many wonders and signs performed by the apostles. All the believers were together and had everything in common. They sold property and possessions to give to anyone who had need. Every day they continued to meet together in the temple courts. They broke bread in their homes and ate together with glad and sincere hearts, praising God and enjoying the favor of all the people. And the Lord added to their number daily those who were being saved.[217]

Don't misunderstand: I am not advocating living in a commune. I'm talking about living as a community, a "family" of believers. Notice that they fellowshipped *in each other's homes.*

Paul described this type of unity as a marriage:

For this reason a man will leave his father and mother and be united to his wife, and the two will become one flesh. This is a profound mystery—but I am talking about Christ and the church.[218]

Christ and the church are to be like husband and wife, so close that they are no longer identified as separate individuals, but as one. This is how the Father, Son, and Holy Spirit are three in one: one inseparable entity.[219]

---

217 Acts 2:42–47.

218 Eph 5:31–32.

219 Some Jews argue that Christians follow a different God than they do because Christians believe in the *Trinity* (a word not found in the New Testament). They cite the

This is how Jesus described his relationship with the Father and our relationship with him and the Father.

Paul uses the term *mystery*. This English word does not convey the full meaning of what Paul is discussing. Marriage is a real-life play for the world to see. It represents the same type of relationship Christ has with his bride. It also displays the type of unity that Jesus prayed for all believers to experience.

> I do not pray for these alone, but also for those who will believe in me through their word; that they all may be one, as you, Father, are in me, and I in you; that they also may be one in us, that the world may believe that You sent me. And the glory which you gave me I have given them, that they may be one just as we are one: I in them, and you in me; that they may be made perfect in one, and that the world may know that you have sent me, and have loved them as you have loved me.[220]

Five times in this passage Jesus uses the term "be one," "in one," or "are one." Five times he uses the term "in me," "in you," "in us," or "in them." It is pretty clear that he is praying that the unity that he had with the Father be accomplished in us "on earth, as it is in heaven."

WE NEED THIS TYPE OF RELATIONSHIP IN THE ELDERSHIP.

Elders must struggle with very personal and sometimes divisive issues. They are privy to information that the congregation does not have. Much like a doctor or attorney, they are the custodians of information

---

Shema (Dt 6:4) "Hear, O Israel: The LORD our God, the LORD is one." Although this is true in relation to the worship of multiple gods by pagans, it does not account for the perfect unity of the Father, Son and Holy Spirit. They are the one, True God. Just as God created mankind (male and female) "in our" image to be "one flesh," the church will be one with Christ.

220 Jn 17:20–23.

that either should not be public or should only be public given the proper context and timing. This requires elders to adhere to strict confidentiality within the confines of secular law.

I use the marriage analogy because it represents the kind of commitment needed within the eldership to function properly. For example, it is destructive for a mother and father to discuss discipline issues in front of their child, especially if the issue is related to another child. It also gives the child the opportunity to take the side of one parent over the other. Elders' deliberations must take place for the right answer to be acquired, but the process itself may be misinterpreted by a third party.

Worse still is when a husband and wife discuss their marriage in front of their children. In addition to misunderstanding, it creates a real sense of insecurity in the child. These examples can be applied to the eldership. Certain issues should only be discussed with those who have the responsibility, intimacy, and assurance of commitment.

The benefits of confidentiality within the eldership are many. First, a vigorous discussion between Mom and Dad may appear to be a "fight" in the eyes of the child. Without the assurance that discussions will be kept confidential, elders will be less likely to speak their minds. This is the reason that men of experience, wisdom, and character are selected. They have been through these types of discussions with their wives and others for a number of years and know how "to speak the truth in love."

Additionally, elders are selected to handle issues that the congregation cannot handle as a whole without causing great division. Even if division is not the result, these issues will unnecessarily drain the congregation's time and energy. If the congregation has to vote or enter into every issue that the elders deal with, the work of the church will come to a standstill.

Since a congregation encompasses believers of all levels of maturity, by definition it will not have the marriage-like commitment of the eldership. Keep in mind that in all congregations, there are "seekers" who are still not believers, and as Jesus warned, there may also be false teachers who masquerade as wolves in sheep's clothing.

There were many followers of Jesus, but he selected only twelve to disciple. In John chapter 15, Jesus calls his disciples "friends." He says, "I no longer call you servants, because a servant does not know his master's business. Instead, I have called you friends, for everything that I learned from my Father I have made known to you." When did the disciples transition from servants to friends?

There were even different levels of intimacy within the disciples. Jesus only took Peter, John, and James (the brother of John) with him to the Mount of Transfiguration.

> As they were coming down the mountain, Jesus instructed them, "Don't tell anyone what you have seen, until the Son of Man has been raised from the dead."[221]

In saying *don't tell anyone,* Jesus was including the rest of the disciples. Why? One answer may be that Judas was one of the twelve, but I don't think that was it. These three were leaders of the disciples after Jesus's resurrection, until Herod killed James. Peter and John continued to be leaders. Maybe Jesus knew they needed this experience to encourage the others until he was resurrected.

---

221 Mt 17:9.

CHAPTER 21

Kingston upon Thames, a Good Example

<figure>ornament</figure>

From 1974 to 1976, I led a Christian rock band called Liberation Suite. We spent time in Belfast, Northern Ireland, and then we moved to London. While we were there, we met members of a church in Kingston upon Thames, which is close to London. Since it was not far from our home in Surrey, we became part of their fellowship. It was our home away from home.

This church did not have a "Pastor." Instead, there were four elders. Most of the leaders and congregants came out of the Church of England. The first thing we noticed about the church was its lack of hierarchy. One of the elders and his wife were well-known actors. Although he was viewed by most as the chief elder, he never allowed himself or anyone else to give him any title different from the other elders. In fact, he staunchly rejected such a role, even though he appeared to have the most wisdom and experience. He worked closely with the other elders. The only other elder I remember well was a flamboyant man from Nigeria.

This church numbered about 150, and they met on Sundays in the local school gym. When we arrived at the meeting, there was no call to order or opening prayer. The people walked in singing. Some played guitars while others had tambourines. The worship was free-flowing and heartfelt. It continued until there was a natural lull. At that point, people prayed silently or publicly. Others would voice a word from God or read from God's Word. Normally, there would be an ebb and flow of worship interspersed with mini sermons. Usually, the Nigerian elder would speak with great fervor and passion, and the old actor would speak with hushed wisdom. However, at other times, neither would speak, and someone else would bring forth a message. It was refreshing and uplifting.

To some this may sound like chaos, but not to me. The people appeared to be led by the Spirit. They moved from song to song and message to message "in a fitting and orderly way," as Paul had instructed the Corinthians. They did not step on each other's toes. They sat down when someone else had something to say. This kind of relationship comes about only through the effective, gentle example of the elders themselves, who did not seek their own way.

Paul explains this in 1 Corinthians 14:30–33:

> What then shall we say, brothers? When you come together, everyone has a hymn, or a word of instruction, a revelation, a tongue or an interpretation....All of these must be done for the strengthening of the church. But everything should be done in a fitting and orderly way.[222]

I don't know of a church in America that functions like the one Paul described but I'm sure there are. Admittedly, I have not tried to seek them out. The closest I personally encountered was this church in Kingston.

Was the worship perfect? Probably not. No worship and no institution of man are perfect; but this leadership and worship experience most closely resembled the leadership and worship gathering that I read about in the New Testament.

I don't know if this kind of meeting can occur in groups much larger than the one I encountered; however, my guess is that the larger the congregation, the greater the need for maturity and submission by the people to the Holy Spirit.

---

222 1 Cor 14:26, 40.

The early churches of the New Testament met in homes or outside. Most believers were under duress either from their pagan neighbors, the disbelieving Jews, or the government itself. There was only one church in Jerusalem, and it numbered many thousands. There were three thousand added on the day of Pentecost to those already in the church, and Acts says people were added daily. As far as we know, there were no permanent buildings. This is how believers meet in countries like China today where they are persecuted.

In London during the mid-1970s, there was a strong home-church movement. The Kingston church periodically joined with these churches to rent the Royal Albert Hall in London, which then seated about seven thousand people. They would meet together to hear from the prophets and other leaders and join in collective worship. The one I attended was very uplifting. The worship and dance glorified God. We also heard from Malcolm Muggridge, who was the Walter Cronkite of England. He had recently been converted after living most of his life as an avowed atheist.

Churches in America will not always be able to publicly support megachurches and their multimillion-dollar programs. I do not think large churches are bad; they serve a purpose. However, I think that they tend to demand a hierarchy that leads to the priest/king or CEO-type Pastor. As stated earlier, what the world and the church really need is a family, pastored and overseen by loving elders.

Most churches have acknowledged that it's impossible to relate to individual needs when the church grows beyond a certain point. Therefore, they have adopted some form of small group meeting during the week, usually in homes. These may be called family groups, heart groups, or promise groups, but their purpose seems to be the same: touch the people.

All too often, the church hierarchy uses these small group meetings to hand down a syllabus from the Pastor or require a discussion of the Pastor's last sermon. This is OK if you think the Pastor is the source of all teaching and inspiration. It is not in keeping with what Paul says should happen. "When you come together, everyone has a hymn, or a word of instruction, a revelation, a tongue or an interpretation....All of these must be done for the strengthening of the church. For you can all prophesy in turn so that everyone may be instructed and encouraged."

Why can't the elder, who may be a plumber, speak to the congregation? As I recall, Peter was a fisherman and a pretty good preacher, too. These meetings are also a great opportunity for young people and those "new to the way" to learn to speak, pray, and lead group discussions while making mistakes. The group leader, an elder or other senior church member, can graciously monitor and train these "youngsters" in the Lord. Once they learn to move in concert with the order of the Holy Spirit in small groups, they are more able to discern the movement of the Holy Spirit in meetings of the entire church. Once again, Paul is expecting something supernatural (higher than the natural) to happen. The natural order of a service requires a bulletin, rehearsals, and other preparations. This is not always wrong, but it is wrong if it is always done this way. When does the Holy Spirit get to talk to and through his people?

(For a further discussion of the worship experience in an elder-led church, see chapter 27.)

Section 7—How Does This Work?

"IF IT QUACKS LIKE A DUCK" is a guide for evaluating your own church leadership structure. One subtle change can make a fundamental difference. Many churches that profess to be elder led also have Pastors. In reality, they are similar to my former church: a Pastor-run church with an advisory board of elders.

"Qualifications of Elders and Deacons" gives more insight into the purposes of the qualifications. It also gives more attention to the office of deacon.

The chapter "Duties of an Eldership" discusses the primary duties of elders—to oversee and care for (pastor, shepherd) the local church. This involves elements of leadership, teaching, and personal ministry.

In "Just the FAQs," I answer many of the obvious questions you may have, such as: How do we select elders? Can an elder resign, retire, or be fired?

Elders are not appointed for life. They are appointed for as long as they remain qualified. Qualification involves more than just the character and experience requirements, it also includes the aspiration and drive to commit to the work (ergon) of the eldership. This chapter also discusses the aspect of discipline when "caring for" and "overseeing" the church.

CHAPTER 22

If It Quacks Like a Duck

❦

I use the example of my former church, which still considers itself to be an elder-led church. In fact, it is a Pastor-led church with a Pastor's "board of advisors." Shortly after ordaining elders in the early 1970s, the church elevated one of the elders to be the only full-time Pastor. This change didn't seem fundamental at the time, since the elder was already ordained by his former denomination as a Pastor. From that time until now, the church has always selected a Pastor from outside the eldership and from outside the church.

EVIDENCE THAT YOU DON'T HAVE AN ELDER-LED CHURCH

This chapter applies only to those churches that *profess* to be led by elders. They are notably in the minority, even for those committed to a strict adherence to the scripture. There are fewer still that are *actually* led by elders.

Most churches and old denominations do not even pretend to be led by elders. Of course, the Catholic hierarchy is well known. So, also, are the Methodists and other main-line Protestant denominations. Some Baptists are independent, in that each church "calls" its own Pastor rather than have one appointed by a regional hierarchy. However, the Pastor and his staff clearly run the independent Baptist church unless the deacons (church board) replace them. Of the denominations with which I am familiar, only the Presbyterians profess to be elder run, but even they are Pastor led when you examine them according to the criteria that follow.

There may be others, of which I am unaware, that operate according to the teachings of Paul regarding New Testament church government. However, my goal in this chapter is not to examine and evaluate the structure of every denomination. My goal is to point out the scriptures that clearly call for elder government and to identify its benefits and characteristics. Then you, should you aspire to be an elder, can evaluate your own leadership to see what you have.

FRANCHISE CHURCHES

The nondenominational Charismatic movement is also characterized by a strong Pastoral authority. Some churches have even established regional and national hierarchies after reproducing their church brand in other cities and states. This is similar to opening a retail franchise. If you want to use the name, you have to play by the rules of the corporate office. Because they are not truly independent, these churches look to the home church as their overseers. This tends to limit the local cooperation with other churches that is needed to represent the whole Christ in each community. I have seen this in my home town, where a local Pastor has ties to the mother church in another city. In my opinion, this is another obstacle that would prevent his church from truly uniting with others in our town. Of course, it's not nearly as limiting as the old denominations having national hierarchies.

LOOK AT THE SIGNS.

Many churches have organizational charts, just like businesses. There's nothing wrong with that. You may say that your church doesn't have an "org chart." I would answer that while you may not have one printed on paper, every regular attendee has one printed in his or her mind. It is regularly reinforced from the sign on the front of the church to the bulletin handed to you at the door to the website and Facebook page. (See chapter 27 for a list of other things that must change to become an elder-led church.)

One of the first projects I had as a college business major was to prepare an org chart for a local business. My assignment was to interview upper management and then the frontline employees. I selected a bank. After conducting interviews, I was to draw an org chart based on my interviews and compare them with the official org chart that the business had created. The results were revealing. The president and vice presidents described an organization that was pretty close to the structure represented by the official org chart. However, the chart derived from interviews with the tellers was not the same. This is true in every organization, whether it is a school, a business, or a church—there is an *official* org chart and a *de facto* org chart. The de facto chart is what most people respond to.

Why are there such discrepancies? Most management experts will tell us that a well-managed organization has a unified vision. Not every employee may know all the details, but they know what the purpose of the organization is and what their role is in fulfilling that purpose. Organizations and churches that have a wide disparity between the stated purpose and the common perception are not well managed.

Sometimes this disparity occurs when management changes direction and does not communicate its philosophy shift to the rank and file. However, a worse situation occurs when management changes direction but doesn't realize a change has occurred. In such situations, rank-and-file employees and clients know what the true direction and structure is.

This is also common with churches. The Pastor may profess a direction or mission, but the congregation and visitors have a different impression based on what is actually happening.

YOU CAN'T SEE THE CONTINENTAL DRIFT.

A small change over time can cause a fundamental shift that is difficult to reverse.

My home church members in the early 1970s sought diligently to follow New Testament principles. We originally called ourselves *The New Testament Church*. This desire for scriptural integrity led our leaders to recognize the power of the Holy Spirit and the supernatural gifts of healing, prophecy, and others. It was therefore no coincidence that they also established a leadership council of elders in accordance with Paul's instructions to Timothy and Titus.

Our first deviation from the New Testament was when we designated one of the elders as *Pastor*. The church paid him to be a full-time minister. He had already been an ordained Baptist Pastor. Over the years, other paid staff members were added.

When the first Pastor left, instead of selecting someone from their own ranks to serve as Pastor, the elders "called" other men to join the eldership and serve as Pastor. With each successive change in Pastors, the elders found themselves to be less independent, functioning more like a board of directors. Their role as shepherds, teachers, and overseers became less than hands-on, instead deferring (or abdicating) to the professional Pastor and his staff until the org chart looked like this:

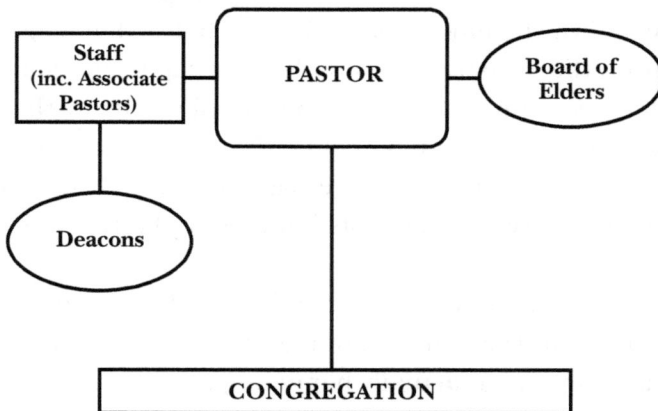

The current Pastor said we had not changed, but if you had asked anyone in the congregation to draw an org chart for our church, it would have looked like the chart above. We even added an associate pastor, which is not a position mentioned in the New Testament. Still worse, the congregation didn't really know what role the elders filled. In some cases, they saw us as an unneeded extra level of bureaucracy that was an impediment to the Pastor. That's what happens when the people are not taught and do not see the elders functioning as elders.

If your org chart doesn't look like the following, you don't have an elder-led church:

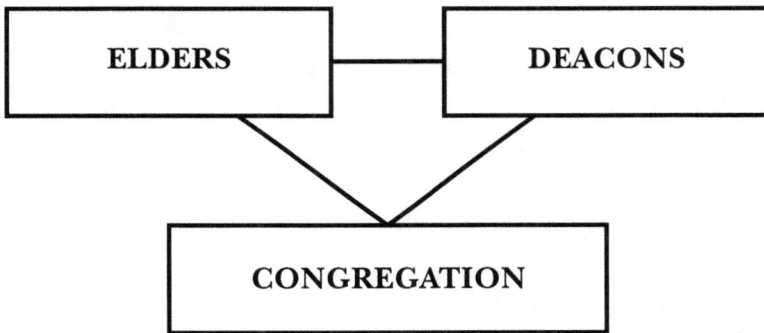

```
┌──────────────┐        ┌──────────────┐
│   ELDERS     │────────│   DEACONS    │
└──────────────┘        └──────────────┘
          ┌────────────────────┐
          │   CONGREGATION     │
          └────────────────────┘
```

LOOK A LITTLE DEEPER.

After I finished what I thought was my last draft of this book, I looked around the Internet to see what churches say about their leadership structure. I was pleased and surprised to find sites where the writer has correctly interpreted the New Testament regarding the issue of leadership by a council of elders. Some churches even have a constitution or bylaws stating that their church is overseen by elders.

However, when I looked a little deeper, I noticed that they don't really practice what they profess. For example, one church had designations for Pastors *and* elders. The Pastors' pictures and biographies were on the church's website, but there was no mention of the elders. Even though the constitution said the church was led by the elders, it was obvious that the day-to-day work of the ministry was being done by the paid Pastors. The constitution required the "Senior Pastor" to be an elder. It is obvious that the elders at best function like a corporate board of directors without being involved in the daily work of the ministry. More likely, they serve as a pastoral advisory board, as our elders did. The Senior Pastor and "his" staff (the other Pastors) truly do the heavy lifting. If the elders do not perform the work of the ministry, as in the early church, other positions must be delegated to do that work. That is what has happened in so many churches. If it quacks like a Pastor-led church, it is.

What Is the Purpose of Your Elders?

If your church has a group of elders and deacons, what do they do? Don't say what you *think* they should be doing. Evaluate what they *actually do*. In my former church, you would have been hard-pressed to find someone who could explain exactly what our elders did. That would not have been the case in the early years.

Church members are all familiar with the top-down leadership style of the Gentiles. That's why they readily accept and defend Pastor rule. They have not been taught about biblical church leadership and elders. Those who have been taught are told that *Pastor* is synonymous with *elder*. No one seems to question why there is only one Elder/Pastor.

If the church has men who are trying to function as elders, they will encounter opposition from the Pastor and the congregation unless the Pastor is committed to stepping down and teaching the congregation about New Testament leadership.

When elders are not established in their scriptural role in the church, the congregation views them as usurping the Pastor's role if they try to pastor the congregation through preaching and teaching. Worse still, the congregation could view them as rebellious, having no respect for "God's man." This produces contempt for the eldership. At the very least, they will be viewed as an unnecessary additional level of bureaucracy.

WHO ESTABLISHES THE ELDERS?

If the Pastor selects your elders, they are not an eldership and you do not have an elder-led church. (See chapter 25 for a more in-depth discussion on elder selection.)

WHO DECIDES MAJOR DOCTRINAL ISSUES?

As undershepherds of the Lord, elders are there to protect the flock from heresy and false teachers. Paul and Jude exhorted the brethren to contend for the faith. *Contend* comes from the same root word as *fight*. We are not to be contentious. However, there are some things worth fighting for. The gospel is one of those things.

Remember how vigorously Paul argued with the circumcision party over his contention that Gentiles should not be required to be circumcised. This was an issue of faith, not obedience. It would have been much easier for him to have them circumcised. If he had done this, their confidence would have been in their obedience to regulations rather than the grace of God. This is the type of doctrinal issue that a council of elders must answer. In a Pastor-run church, the church's teaching and emphasis is susceptible to change every time the Pastor changes.

WHO DEFINES AND COMMUNICATES CHURCH VISION?

If the Pastor is the only one who communicates the vision, you are not an elder-led church. Jesus gave his disciples the mission, direction, and vision of the church just prior to his ascension. Although, Jesus personally told Peter to "care for my sheep," other apostles and elders, such as James and John, were prominent leaders at other important times.

187

How each local church fulfills its mission should be established by the council of elders with continual input from church members. Anything else indicates you don't have an elder-led church.

CHAPTER 23

Qualifications of Elders and Deacons

❧

E lders and deacons are the only two church "offices" to which qualified men may be appointed. In Acts, the "apostles and elders" appointed seven men as deacons to assist them.[223] In Philippians, Paul
greets the "overseers and deacons." In 1 Timothy, he gives the qualifications for deacons immediately after the qualifications for elders.

> Here is a trustworthy saying: If anyone sets his heart (oregomai)
> on being an overseer (episcope), he desires a noble task (ergon).[224]

Following are the Greek definitions of the terms mentioned above. [225]

Aspires or Desires—*orego* (3977)
To set one's heart on, strive for, aspire to, desire, to extend,
stretch out; to stretch one's self out, to reach forward to, to desire
earnestly, long after, to indulge in, be devoted to.

Task or Work—*ergon* (2240)
Work, deed, activity, job, duty, office, charge, business.

---

223 Acts 6:3–4.
224 1 Tm 3:1; emphasis added.
225 Goodrick-Kohlenberger numbering system.

Elders hold the only church leadership position to which men with the following qualifications may apply or aspire.

Elders must first be men of personal integrity. Second, they must be men whose management, leadership, and oversight skills have been tested successfully. Where are these skills tested? They are tested at home with daily decisions over finances, education, discipline, and doctrine: all the issues of life. Just as David learned courage by protecting his father's sheep from the lion and bear, elders learn how to "rule" the family of God by "ruling" their own households. Paul made this very clear in his letter to Timothy about the qualifications of elders:

> He must manage his own family well and see that his children obey him, and he must do so in a manner worthy of full respect. (If anyone does not know how to manage his own family, how can he take care of God's church?)[226]

If elders have managed their own families well, they have something valuable to bring to the table when it comes to managing God's house. Today, it is becoming harder to meet this requirement because of divorce and children from different parents living in the same household.

Each elder must

- accept his role;
- know that he hears from God;
- be willing to speak up;
- be willing to be wrong; and
- be willing for others to be wrong.

---

226 1 Tm 3:4–5.

QUALIFY YOURSELVES

In chapter 15 we discussed two lessons in which Paul used the analogy of a pot or vessel.

In Romans chapter 9, Paul uses the analogy of a pot questioning the potter as to why he made him a certain way. The idea is that God creates us for specific purposes, and we should accept it and try to determine the specific gifts he has given us to achieve those purposes. This is true of our *gifts*, which God himself distributes, but not our *character.*

If the office of elder may not be obtained on the basis of a man's gift, how does he qualify? Paul uses the same analogy of a pot (vessel) in 2 Tim 2:20–21, but with a different conclusion.

> In a large house there are articles not only of gold and silver, but also of wood and clay; some are for special purposes and some for common use. Those who cleanse themselves from the latter will be instruments for special purposes, made holy, useful to the Master and prepared to do any good work.[227]

We are not born with good character. Paul says that becoming an elder is a *noble task to seek.* Therefore, we must purify ourselves for this duty—purge ourselves from the filth within so that we may perform the honorable works of God.

QUALIFICATIONS OF ELDERS

Paul's letters to Timothy and Titus contain the basic texts for discussing qualifications of elders and deacons. Timothy and Titus both served as apostles and coworkers with Paul. There were other apostles, such as Apollos, Barnabas, and Silas, but Timothy and Titus worked under Paul's tutelage.

---

227 2 Tm 2:20–21.

PAUL'S INSTRUCTION TO TIMOTHY

Here is a trustworthy saying: If anyone sets his heart on being an overseer, he desires a noble task. Now the overseer must be above reproach, the husband of but one wife, temperate, self-controlled, respectable, hospitable, able to teach, not given to drunkenness, not violent but gentle, not quarrelsome, not a lover of money. He must manage his own family well and see that his children obey him with proper respect. (If anyone does not know how to manage his own family, how can he take care of God's church?) He must not be a recent convert, or he may become conceited and fall under the same judgment as the devil. He must also have a good reputation with outsiders, so that he will not fall into disgrace and into the devil's trap.[228]

PAUL'S INSTRUCTION TO TITUS

To Titus, my true son in our common faith: Grace and peace from God the Father and Christ Jesus our Savior.

The reason I left you in Crete was that you might straighten out what was left unfinished and appoint elders in every town, as I directed you. An elder must be blameless, the husband of but one wife, a man whose children believe and are not open to the charge of being wild and disobedient.

Since an overseer is entrusted with God's work, he must be blameless—not overbearing, not quick-tempered, not given to drunkenness, not violent, not pursuing dishonest gain. Rather he must be hospitable, one who loves what is good, who is self-controlled, upright, holy and disciplined. He must hold firmly to the trustworthy message as it has been taught, so that he

---

228 1 Tm 3:1–7.

can encourage others by sound doctrine and refute those who oppose it.[229]

Let's recap the qualifications for elder:

1. be blameless, respectable, and above reproach
2. have a good reputation with outsiders
3. be the husband of one wife
4. be temperate; not quick-tempered; not quarrelsome
5. be self-controlled; not addicted to alcohol (or drugs); not greedy
6. be hospitable
7. be gentle; not violent
8. hold firmly to the gospel and the scriptures
9. be able to teach sound doctrine
10. be able to refute false doctrine
11. manage his own family well; his children should be obedient believers, not wild and disobedient, and his wife should be a woman worthy of respect
12. be a lover of good; be holy and upright

Additionally, an elder must not be a recent convert. Otherwise, he may become conceited and prideful. The term *elder (presbyteros),* by definition, means an older man, presumably with wisdom, stature, and a proven track record.

THE ABILITY TO TEACH AND REFUTE FALSE DOCTRINE

A first this seems to require that each elder must have the *gift* of teaching. Although, as I have stated previously, pastors and teachers should be on the eldership; I don't think this is a requirement that every elder

---

229 Ti 1:4–9.

have the gift of teaching. I think it is more along the line of what Paul told Timothy about how to handle doctrine.

> Warn them before God against quarreling about words; it is of no value, and only ruins those who listen. Do your best to present yourself to God as one approved, a worker who does not need to be ashamed and who correctly handles the word of truth. Avoid godless chatter, because those who indulge in it will become more and more ungodly. Their teaching will spread like gangrene.[230]

Obviously, every elder must be able to comprehend the scriptures. However, teaching others well is a gift. Every elder must:

1. Be a student of the Word. He must study the Word in order to recognize false doctrine.
2. Have a desire to learn more.
3. Be able to interpret the scriptures with clarity and wisdom
4. Correctly handle the word of truth. King James says to "rightly divide the Word of truth."

The last point is in keeping with Paul's warning to avoid godless chatter and quarreling about words. This is what I call having the wisdom to "major on the majors and minor on the minors." Without that wisdom, the church can waste its time and cause divisions over unimportant issues. This gets the church entangled and prevents it from accomplishing the purposes of God.

QUALIFICATIONS OF DEACONS

> Deacons, likewise, are to be men worthy of respect, sincere, not indulging in much wine, and not pursuing dishonest gain.

---

230 2 Tm 2:14-17.

They must keep hold of the deep truths of the faith with a clear conscience. They must first be tested; and then if there is nothing against them, let them serve as deacons.

In the same way, their wives are to be women worthy of respect, not malicious talkers but temperate and trustworthy in everything.

A deacon must be the husband of but one wife and must manage his children and his household well. Those who have served well gain an excellent standing and great assurance in their faith in Christ Jesus.[231]

Deacons and their families have virtually the same character standards as elders. Unlike elders, deacons are not required to teach and refute false doctrine. Since the work they perform is primarily administrative, they free up the elders to teach and shepherd the church.

The apostles in Jerusalem said to select as deacons men "who are known to be full of the Spirit and wisdom." The deacons' first task was to allocate the daily food distribution between the Jewish and Greek widows. This is one of those jobs that require wisdom. This issue of food distribution was very contentious. It had become so time-consuming for the apostles and elders that it was interfering with their primary purpose, which was to minister God's Word.[232] Deacons are indispensable to the harmonious operation of the local church. They are not just maintenance men; they are men of discernment and wisdom.

Paul's requirements for deacons do not include the prohibition against being a recent convert. Paul adds the requirement that they be "tested" to see if there is anything against them. Presumably, elders have been around a while and they are well known by the church. In not requiring deacons to be longtime converts, Paul may have been willing for them to be younger men. That could explain the reason for testing them. They needed a "background check" or on-the-job training before they could be officially appointed as deacons.

---

231 1 Tm 3:8–13.
232 Acts 6:1–4.

An obvious advantage of allowing younger men to serve as deacons is that those with the ability to teach and preach can be observed and later elevated to the position of elder. It is a perfect place of service to "test" their character. Jesus made this point in his parable of the talents when the master commended the servant who had increased his talents. "Well done, good and faithful servant! You have been faithful with a few things; I will put you in charge of many things."[233]

---

233 Mt 25:23.

CHAPTER 24

Duties of Eldership

❧

An elder has no role without the other elders. This is not the job of one man, whether you give him the title of "Pastor," Bishop," "Priest," or "Elder."

The primary role of the eldership is to pastor, shepherd *(poimen)*, and oversee the church. Following is Paul's final charge to the elders of Ephesus when he knew he would no longer see them:

> From Miletus, Paul sent to Ephesus for the elders (presbyteros) of the church.[234]
>
> Keep watch over yourselves and all the flock (poimnion) of which the Holy Spirit has made you overseers (episkopos). Be shepherds (poimaino) of the church of God, which he bought with his own blood.[235]

The last sentence literally means, "Shepherd the church."

Just as the Old Testament used the metaphor of the shepherd to describe the spiritual leaders of Israel, Jesus and his disciples used it to describe the duties and character of church leaders.

---

234 Acts 20:17; emphasis added.
235 Acts 20:28; emphasis added.

1. Shepherds lay down their lives for their sheep.

Jesus said that he, "The Good Shepherd," lays down his life for the sheep. David took on the bear and the lion for his father's sheep. Later, David took on Goliath for his Father's sheep (Israel).

This requires courage, the willingness to die for others. More importantly, it means the willingness to *live* for others, which is more difficult. Jesus challenged his disciples to take a lower position and wash one another's feet. This involves picking up your cross daily and dying to your own desires in favor of others.[236]

2. Shepherds put in long hours out in the field.

Shepherds are out in the field with the sheep usually doing their work outside of the spotlight. Many people may never see or know all the things that pastors (shepherds) do.

Study, counsel, teach, preach, pray, console, discipline. These are just a few of the works of elders. They are continual and inconvenient. An elder is always on call. This is why one man cannot do this for the whole church. If he tries, he will have to "hire" assistant pastors to do some of it. There are no assistant elders. As Paul said, they are the shepherds; they must "pastor" the church.

3. Shepherds feed and care for the lambs and sheep.

Paul made it clear that teaching and preaching are two of the primary duties of shepherds.

> The elders who direct the affairs of the church well are worthy of double honor, especially those whose work is preaching and teaching.[237]

---

236 Lk 9:23.
237 1 Tm 5:17.

After Jesus's resurrection, he appeared to Peter and asked him three times if he loved him. Peter replied each time that he loved Jesus. Jesus commanded Peter to "feed my lambs," "take care of my sheep," and finally, "feed my sheep."[238] The word *poimen* encompasses much more than just feeding. It covers everything needed to "take care of" the sheep: safety, shelter, food, water, rest, and direction.

Jesus asked Peter, as one of the leaders of the apostles and elders, to prove his love by taking care of Jesus's bride, the church.

4. Shepherds protect the flock from predators.

Shepherds must confront false doctrine. This, too, is a responsibility of the eldership. Jude, the half brother of Jesus, called us to "contend for the faith" against "ungodly people, who pervert the grace of our God into a license for immorality." Our Pastors should be preaching this message today instead of one of tolerance toward sinful lifestyles.

In Galatians, Paul vigorously defended the doctrine of salvation by faith against the Judaizers, who taught that Gentiles should also follow the laws of Moses to be justified. Just be sure you are protecting God's people and not "splitting the baby" (sacrificing God's people) to protect your own position.

Jesus warned the large crowd of followers at the Sermon on the Mount about false prophets. He said the sheep may not recognize them as wolves, since they are disguised as sheep, but with discernment, one can tell them by their fruit.

> Watch out for false prophets. They come to you in sheep's clothing, but inwardly they are ferocious wolves. By their fruit you will recognize them...every good tree bears good fruit, but a bad tree bears bad fruit. Thus, by their fruit you will recognize them.[239]

---

238 Jn 21:15–17.
239 Mt 7:15–20.

Paul continues the theme in his farewell address to the elders at Ephesus. Paul includes an additional warning by telling the elders to "Keep watch over *yourselves*" in addition to the flock. This is a key point. What better way to lead the church astray than to infiltrate the leadership itself? That way not only is Christ discredited and misrepresented, so is the church leadership.

> Keep watch over yourselves and all the flock of which the Holy Spirit has made you overseers. Be shepherds of the church of God, which he bought with his own blood. I know that after I leave, savage wolves will come in among you and will not spare the flock. Even from your own number men will arise and distort the truth in order to draw away disciples after them. So be on your guard! Remember that for three years I never stopped warning each of you night and day with tears.[240]

Here is Peter's warning on false teachers and prophets:

> But there were also false prophets among the people, just as there will be false teachers among you. They will secretly introduce destructive heresies, even denying the sovereign Lord who bought them—bringing swift destruction on themselves. Many will follow their depraved conduct and will bring the way of truth into disrepute. In their greed these teachers will exploit you with fabricated stories. Their condemnation has long been hanging over them, and their destruction has not been sleeping.[241]

It is much easier to lead one man astray than it is a group of committed men. As a hunter, I know how difficult it is to approach animals in a herd as opposed to a single animal. The single animal has two eyes, two ears, and one nose to detect predators. When you have a group of

---

240 Acts 20:28–31.
241 2 Pt 2:1–3.

ten, twelve, or more, it is virtually impossible to get close to a herd without being detected. Even if the wind is in your favor, it only takes one of the group to get a glimpse of your movement or hear a twig break. If it does, it sounds the alarm and the rest are alerted. It is almost always the older animals, usually the females with young, that sound the alarm first. That's why men should listen to their wives' intuition.

Elders have safety in numbers if they trust each other's instincts. They are like watchmen along the city walls. If they detect something and fail to alert the city, they are responsible for the result. Read God's warning to Ezekiel about a watchman's responsibility for others.[242] Elders also have safety in a diversity of views. This is also relevant to the family. My wife sometimes spots a fraud or a lie before I do, because she sees things differently than I do. Children need two parents to raise them effectively.

Elders, like all of us, need to trust their instincts and the Holy Spirit within them. They must be discriminating. Being discriminating used to mean being wise and choosing the best. Jesus said to judge them by their fruit. This can be very difficult sometimes, when other people are enamored of a new teacher and a "new" way of teaching. If not detected early, great harm and division can be brought into the church.

Sometimes the predator arises from within the ranks. Paul says that men from your own numbers will arise and seek to draw away disciples to themselves.[243] This is the essence of pride: splitting the Body of Christ to satisfy some perverse need to be a leader. This is the original sin of Lucifer. His disciples continue his example.

5. Shepherds know where they are going.

Jesus said he only did what he saw the Father doing.

Shepherds lead the sheep to green pastures, good water, and a safe resting place. They must know where the Good Shepherd is leading, otherwise the sheep will die along the way.

---

242 Ez 3:17–21.
243 Acts 20:30.

Elders must have a sense of direction for the church. Obviously, they know the Lord's basic teachings and commandments to love one another, but they need specific directions for their time and place. This is where churches get off track. For example, I have seen Pastors use a building campaign as a means to generate church interest. This is an exceptionally bad idea, especially if the church already has significant debt, which is frequently the case.

I've heard it said that a good ox-team driver can get oxen to pull a heavily loaded cart up a hill without a sweat, but a poor driver can exhaust them on the way down. A wise and experienced eldership knows when and where to invest the talents, energy, and financial resources of a church.

There is nothing more demoralizing than to have a Pastor invest time, money, and energy into a project that is doomed to failure from the start. This is usually because the idea was *his* idea and not God's. Elders must be careful to be about God's business, not their own. This requires prayer, discernment, and the counsel of others.

6. Shepherds need to exercise discipline.

This is one of the least discussed and most misunderstood roles of an eldership. Sometimes, being a watchman and sounding the alarm is not enough. Sometimes, there are false brethren who will not respond.

Peter describes some of these people. He calls them false teachers and false prophets.

> Bold and arrogant...these people blaspheme in matters they do not understand. They are like unreasoning animals, creatures of instinct, born only to be caught and destroyed, and like animals they too will perish.
>
> They will be paid back with harm for the harm they have done. Their idea of pleasure is to carouse in broad daylight. They are blots and blemishes, reveling in their pleasures while they feast with you. With eyes full of adultery, they never stop

sinning; they seduce the unstable; they are experts in greed—an accursed brood! They have left the straight way and wandered off to follow the way of Balaam son of Bezer, who loved the wages of wickedness.[244]

Jude also warns the believers:

Dear friends...certain individuals whose condemnation was written about long ago have secretly slipped in among you. They are ungodly people, who pervert the grace of our God into a license for immorality and deny Jesus Christ our only Sovereign and Lord.[245]

Paul commanded the Corinthians to put such a person out of fellowship for sleeping with his father's wife. He appealed to the church as a whole:

It is actually reported that there is sexual immorality among you, and of a kind that even pagans do not tolerate: A man is sleeping with his father's wife. And you are proud! Shouldn't you rather have gone into mourning and have put out of your fellowship the man who has been doing this. For my part, even though I am not physically present, I am with you in spirit. As one who is present with you in this way, I have already passed judgment in the name of our Lord Jesus on the one who has been doing this. So when you are assembled and I am with you in spirit, and the power of our Lord Jesus is present, hand this man over to Satan for the destruction of the flesh, so that his spirit may be saved on the day of the Lord.

Your boasting is not good. Don't you know that a little yeast leavens the whole batch of dough?...I wrote to you in my letter not to associate with sexually immoral people—not at

244   2 Pt 2:10–15.
245   Jude 1:3–4.

all meaning the people of this world who are immoral, or the greedy and swindlers, or idolaters. In that case you would have to leave this world. But now I am writing to you that you must not associate with anyone who claims to be a brother or sister but is sexually immoral or greedy, an idolater or slanderer, a drunkard or swindler. Do not even eat with such people.

What business is it of mine to judge those outside the church? Are you not to judge those inside? God will judge those outside. "Expel the wicked person from among you."[246]

---

246 1 Cor 5:1–13.

CHAPTER 25

Just the FAQs

❦

My son called one day and asked me what I was doing. I told him I was writing a book on church leadership. He knew the issues but was unclear on how elder leadership would work. His questions prompted me to write this chapter, in which I attempt to explain my understanding in the simplest way I know.

OVERVIEW

God gives individuals insight into when the church needs emphasis on a particular teaching or *doctrine.* He also gives direction on *church activities,* such as missions, evangelism, and pastoral and counseling ministries. Direction does not always originate from the leadership. Many times elders are approached by others in the congregation to whom God has spoken. Elders must weigh these issues to determine whether they are for the church as a whole or for individuals to pursue.

When an elder receives an insight and is ready to act on it, he should bring it before the other elders. It may be that the other elders immediately identify with the vision because they have been thinking the same thing. This is wonderful; it is nice to experience those times where God confirms the same thing to each person. However, we should not always expect that to happen. Remember, Paul says our understanding is imperfect, like looking through a dark glass. More importantly, as unique individuals, we see an eternal, all-powerful God from many different perspectives. What do we do when five of six elders are in agreement and one is not? This is when elders must operate in a higher than natural (supernatural) manner.

This is not a time for democracy. This is a time for the supernatural. If we believe that each elder hears from God, and we trust his motives and his commitment, we should be willing to hear and understand his concerns. If the one who is opposed respects the judgment and motives of the five, he should be willing to accept that they see something he does not see at this point. If his only objection is that he doesn't think the issue is as important as the other five do, he should be willing to submit to and support their proposal.

However, if the one elder has a strong basis for rejecting the proposal, he should stand his ground. God is fully capable of preventing a mistake with only one man. The five should submit to him and trust his warning. It is possible that he has protected them and the church from making a disastrous decision. It is also possible that the timing is wrong, and if so, the one may agree at a later date. In each case, each elder should state his case and be willing to defer, if possible, to the others. There will be times where deferral is not an option.

Of course this unity will be tested, just as when a child tries to play one parent against the other. When the child is repeatedly unsuccessful in his attempts to divide the parents, he or she reaffirms their authority and unity. It quells most future attempts. So it will be in the church when elders dwell together in unity.

Unity does not mean *unanimity*. That's not what parental unity is about either. Parents submit to one another out of a higher calling to God and because they love their children. So do the elders. Discussion and disagreement are normal and healthy. This is how the other elders know when one has heard from God. He must stick to his guns when God has shown him something important that the others haven't seen. Likewise, the other elders must trust and respect that this man knows God and would not act this way unless he had something important to impart. Remember what Paul said about love: "It always…trusts, [and] always perseveres."[247]

Therefore, it is each elder's responsibility and duty to share what God has shown him, even if he knows there will be those who may not see it. This is the perseverance of love. Likewise, those elders who hear something strange that God has not revealed to them, either because they are not inclined in that direction or because God has just hidden it from them, must show their love by trusting the one with whom they have a covenant.

Without this interaction, there is no learning and no understanding. This is what is missing in Pastor rule. God's will is in the midst of these discussions and disagreements even if his will is just to wait awhile. All elders must conform to Jesus's will and accede to unity in the bond of peace for the sake of his body, just as loving, committed parents do out of love for God and their children. Otherwise, they may be guilty of "splitting the baby."

IT'S LIKE A MARRIAGE COVENANT

Our entire mind-set has to change. Envision the relationship between a husband and wife. At first, the relationship is awkward. Who writes the bills? Who mows the grass? Who cooks and cleans? When a man and a woman have children, they encounter a new set of challenges. Now there are new responsibilities and duties. They adjust. They don't change the husband-wife structure just because the duties change.

In some marriages, the husbands write the bills, while in others, the wife is more capable in this area. So it is in a well-functioning eldership. That is why elders, with input from the congregation, select new elders who complement what is lacking in their skill set and motivations. In some cases, elders take on different duties within their ability. The main difference in the analogy with marriage is that elders are

---

247   1 Cor 13:7; emphasis added.

interchangeable with other qualified men in the church. They may retire or take a sabbatical as needed. Yet all have a covenant with one
another.

No longer is one man required to be the scholar, the priest, the
shepherd, the overseer, and the administrator. Except for the priestly
role, elders are called upon to shepherd the flock individually and collectively by teaching sound doctrine, settling disputes, providing vision
and direction, and protecting them from predators.

The calling of elders is in keeping with Paul's description of love.
Elders must be patient, kind, slow to anger, and humble. They seek the
good of the congregation rather than their own good. They protect the
congregation from threats inside and outside. They are forgiving and do
not hold grudges. They give second and third chances to restore trust
where trust has been violated. They provide guidance and vision and
achieve goals by perseverance with hope and faith.

As I discussed in chapter 19, it is not possible to have an effective
elder-led church without supernatural faith and obedience to Jesus's
command to love one another. I am not talking about when miraculous events occur. I am talking about men behaving and trusting each
other in ways that are "above" the natural. That is the true meaning of
supernatural.

The natural tendency is to withhold our trust. Even in a marriage,
we sometimes withhold our trust from our spouse because we are afraid
of the inevitable hurt or betrayal. This same fear keeps church leaders
from attempting the elder-led model and opting for a more familiar
natural model.[248]

Using the analogy of the husband-wife relationship, many young
men and women want to "try out" the marriage thing by "shacking up"

---

248 That is what the children of Israel did when they insisted that Samuel give them
a king so they could be "like other nations." God told Samuel that they were not rejecting him; they were rejecting God as their king. Subsequently, the nation of Israel
became "like the nations" that God drove out of the land. They adopted practices
even more evil than those of the nations God drove out. Ultimately, God drove the
Israelites out for seventy years.

for a few months or years before deciding to get married. Unfortunately, many have children without the commitment to persevere. When the breakup occurs, everyone gets hurt—especially the children. A church should not enter into elder rule without a commitment to see it through.

It is much easier for one man to set the vision for us all. If it breaks down, then the board of directors just finds another CEO with a new staff to try something new. If we were talking about a college football team, it would be like the alumni pressuring the athletic director to hire a new head coach and coaching staff to start winning. God does not want us to "experiment" on his people until we find the right leadership team. That team is already there.

But what is success and what is winning? Our goal is to show God's love to the world by representing a loving church family. As church leaders, we should exemplify what it means to prefer one another above ourselves. What better place to start than with the leadership? Jesus himself said that leadership in the Kingdom of God is different from leadership in the world. The first is last.

Though many of today's Pastors are committed men, are they unselfish when it comes to releasing their exalted role? Remember the parable Jesus told of the man who took the seat of honor at a banquet and was asked to move to a lower seat? Elders must not seek the seat of honor and Pastors must be willing to move to a different seat. In some cases, that may not even include a seat with the elders.

Now back to marriage. When we married our wives, we gave up our independent life. The scripture says that two lives became one. Likewise, when elders who are leaders as individuals agree to submit to one another out of love and respect for the Lord, they too have made a covenant to act as one. In order for this supernatural relationship to work between men who traditionally are taught to forge their own way, we must submit to one another out of respect for the Lord.

How Do We Select Our First Council of Elders?

There is no biblical record as to how or when elders began working alongside the twelve disciples of Jesus as leaders in the Jerusalem church. James, the half brother of Jesus, was considered an elder. He was one of the most prominent of the apostles and elders, along with Peter and John.[249]

Apostles to the Gentile churches (Paul, Barnabas,[250] Timothy, and Titus) appointed elders in the churches they started. There is no other instruction I am aware of in the New Testament as to how elders should be appointed. (See Appendix C—The Apostle.)

I suggest church members select their initial elders in accordance with Paul's instructions to Timothy and Titus. If there was no apostle who started the church, church members should seek guidance from other churches having a biblical eldership. The following paragraphs describe how an existing council of elders should select replacement elders. In a church with no elders, its members could select a committee to perform the role of the council of elders in nominating, evaluating, and hearing testimony regarding those who express a desire to serve as elders and are found to meet the qualifications.

How Do We Select Replacement Elders?

I see no instruction from Paul as to how to select replacement elders. My *suggestion* is that the elders should solicit a list of nominations from church members. After careful evaluation and interview, the eldership should give the congregation a list of candidates who not only meet the qualifications, but who in the opinion of the elders can work together. Since these men will need to arrive at consensus on major matters, they must be confident that each one has the character and respect for the church and the eldership to function in this manner. As noted in prior chapters, they must not be yes-men; but they must be willing to submit

---

249   Gal 2:9.
250   Acts 14:23.

to each other. A person who always has a strong opinion on every matter, is probably not elder material.

Church members should then be given the opportunity to bring testimony to the eldership concerning each nominee. Hopefully, the lives of the men nominated will already be an "open book." However, if a church member, or even an outsider, has a serious objection, the eldership should listen and corroborate the testimony by one or two other credible witnesses.[251] As discussed later in this chapter, this situation must be handled with much wisdom. If an accusation brought against a *candidate* is validated by the elders, I don't think an explanation is automatically due the congregation, as it would be in the case of dismissing a *sitting* elder.

Once the nomination, evaluation, and testimony phases are complete, the elders (or in the case of a new eldership, the committee) should prayerfully make their selections.

This is how our New Testament Church selected replacement elders. I think it worked fairly well, except for the fact that our elders also instituted a Pastor to head up the eldership. This destroyed the eldership dynamic and caused the elders to become an advisory board. Most times they selected a Pastor who came from outside the eldership and usually from outside the church.

How Do We Make Decisions?

My son asked me two obvious and valid questions. The first was, how do you make decisions? And the second was, is there a chief elder who breaks the tie?

There is one answer to both questions. Before I get to that, I would like to set the stage. We in America tend to think of leadership structures in terms of autocratic or democratic. We in the working world know all too well that we must accept the autocratic style if we want a job. That is true whether we work for business, government, the military, or

---

251   1 Tm 5:19–21.

academia. On the other hand, our political background tells us there is value in people selecting their own leaders. We call that democracy. Although both models have their good points, we are not talking about either here.

Our current Pastor-led model fits the autocratic style. However, I am not advocating a democratic form of church leadership either. Elders should arrive at consensus. Remember, the goal is unity in love, not unanimity.

Does this mean that elders just acquiesce to the others? Absolutely not! Elders who do so *should not be elders.* If they are "yes-men," they have become placeholders and frauds. If each elder does not speak what God has shown him, he is setting the stage for takeover by an autocrat. If we acquiesce to the most forceful elder, that would put us right back in the autocratic model. Only this time it would be worse, because we now say that we are an elder-led church, but we are not.

I found myself in an eldership that was just an advisory board for the Pastor. I told our Pastor and elders that if we didn't want to be an elder-led church, we should be honest and tell people we are a Pastor-led church. I encouraged them to be the best Pastor-led church they could be. They didn't accept that either, so the church members continue in their misunderstanding of elders.

My son's second question was, who breaks the tie? My answer is there is no vote. Elders arrive at consensus. This seems impractical and unreasonable; but it isn't. Husbands and wives do this all the time regarding important decisions such as raising their children, where to live, and where to go to church.

THREE NEGATIVE WAYS CONSENSUS CAN BE VIEWED.

First, the strong and pushy elders overwhelm the less forceful elders to accept their position. This goes back to chapter 19 in which I discussed the natural order and the higher order of relating to one another. Each elder should be courageous enough to stand his ground and be the last man standing when he thinks the stakes are high enough. Otherwise, he should not be an elder.

Second, consensus can be thought of as compromise. Once again, this indicates that the compromising elder didn't care that much about the issue at hand and hopes to have someone compromise later for "his" issue. Compromise smacks of politics and a violation of principle. Elders don't need to be reelected and they don't need the job.

Third, in order to just get along and have harmony in the group, one or more elders may participate in *groupthink*. If so, they are worse than placeholders, because they have taken the seat of someone who could be effective.

> *Groupthink* is a psychological phenomenon that occurs within a group of people, in which the desire for harmony or conformity in the group results in an irrational or dysfunctional decision-making outcome. Group members try to minimize conflict and reach a consensus decision without critical evaluation of alternative viewpoints, by actively suppressing dissenting viewpoints, and by isolating themselves from outside influences.
>
> Loyalty to the group requires individuals to avoid raising controversial issues or alternative solutions, and there is loss of individual creativity, uniqueness and independent thinking. The dysfunctional group dynamics of the "ingroup" produces an "illusion of invulnerability" (an inflated certainty that the right decision has been made). Thus the "ingroup" significantly overrates its own abilities in decision-making, and significantly underrates the abilities of its opponents (the "outgroup"). Furthermore groupthink can produce dehumanizing actions against the "outgroup."[252]

---

252 Wikipedia, http://en.wikipedia.org/wiki/Groupthink.

Should elders always stand by their opinions and never defer to one another? No, if they did, the eldership would be going in circles much of the time.

A Time to Defer

There are definite times when elders should defer:

1) when the issue is not one of major significance;
2) when the solution will not deviate from the scripture; and
3) when a majority of the other elders strongly agree.

In these instances, I say an elder should defer to the conviction of the others and support their decision. The next time, he may be the one who is convinced and others may need to defer to his perspective because they trust his character, even if they don't "get it." This is why it is so important to add men as elders whom you know and whose motivations you trust.

An elder should not defer or acquiesce if he is still absolutely convinced that the decision is wrong and will cause harm. The other elders should respect his concern, because they know he is not just being self-centered and obstinate. The other elders should defer to him, even if he is in the minority, until they are all comfortable with the proposed course of action. It may well be that the timing is wrong or that God has spoken to one man a warning that the others do not hear. I do not believe in majority rule. All major decisions should be made unanimously. This may involve deference by one or more elders; but only under the conditions outlined above.

First Among Equals

In my description of the Kingston church, I mentioned a man who was clearly the wisest and the oldest of the elders. In fact, we visited him for counsel on various issues. He had a humble manner that belied his experience and accomplishments. His counsel gave us confidence.

This man was "first among equals" in the Kingston eldership; yet he vehemently refused to be acknowledged as anything more than a fellow elder.[253] As noted elsewhere, he and others had come out of the Church of England, which has a religious hierarchy that parallels the Roman Catholic Church.

The Book of Acts provides evidence of apostles who could be classified as first among equals. Paul certainly was one. Likewise Peter. The first part of Acts is about the leadership of Peter. The latter part is devoted to Paul's life and work. Paul said Peter was the apostle to the Jews, and he was the apostle to the Gentiles. Peter was chosen by Jesus to be one of his disciples. Likewise, Paul was chosen by the risen Christ. *Neither Peter nor Paul claimed a higher status than any of the other apostles.*

John, who called himself "the disciple whom Jesus loved" because of his intimate relationship with Jesus, claimed no higher position than the other disciples. In his second and third epistles, John refers to himself only as the "elder."

Paul claimed no greater position than the apostle Apollos when rebuking the Corinthians for their divisive practice of identifying themselves as followers of Apollos, of Peter, of Paul, or even of Jesus. Even though Paul established the church in Corinth, he encouraged Apollos to visit them and minister to them.

One of you says, "I follow Paul"; another, "I follow Apollos"; another, "I follow Cephas"; still another, "I follow Christ."[254]

---

253 This elder told me he confronted Derek Prince on his teaching about a "Chief Elder or Shepherd." He said Mr. Prince admitted to him he had no scriptural basis for this teaching. Derek Prince was a world-renowned teacher during the Charismatic movement in the '60s and '70s.

254 1 Cor 1:12.

What, after all, is Apollos? And what is Paul? Only servants, through whom you came to believe—as the Lord has assigned to each his task. [255]

Now, brothers and sisters, I have applied these things to myself and Apollos for your benefit, so that you may learn from us the meaning of the saying, "Do not go beyond what is written." Then you will not be puffed up in being a follower of one of us over against the other. [256]

Peter, James, and John were the "reputed pillars" of the church in Jerusalem.[257] None claimed preeminence. James was the half brother of Jesus. Although he was never a disciple, he became one of the elders of the church in Jerusalem. He spoke on behalf of the apostles and elders in Jerusalem concerning the monumental decision to not require Gentile believers to comply with all the laws of Moses.

"It is my judgment, therefore, that we should not make it difficult for the Gentiles who are turning to God. Instead we should write to them, telling them to abstain from food polluted by idols, from sexual immorality, from the meat of strangled animals and from blood." [258]

In these examples, James, John, Peter, and Paul each had reason to assert their preeminence over the others; yet they did not. They didn't speak of themselves as having any greater position than any of the other apostles or elders.

Each was a gifted leader and stood out from among the other disciples and elders. How did they handle themselves? *They submitted one to another.*

---

255 1 Cor 3:5.
256 1 Cor 4:6.
257 Gal 2:9.
258 Acts 15:13–21.

- Paul submitted to Peter, James, and John in the matter of circumcision.
- Peter and John followed James's lead in announcing the Gentile decision.
- Paul rebuked Peter for not associating with Gentiles, even though he had already been told by God in a vision not to call them unclean.
- Peter referred to Paul's epistles as "scripture."

Wow, what would happen today if our leaders did the same?

CAN AN ELDER BECOME DISQUALIFIED?

Yes. Unlike the gifts of God, which are irrevocable (given without return), the position of elder may be and, in some cases, should be revoked. In simple terms, an elder may retire, resign, or be fired if he no longer has the qualities required for the office.

CAN AN ELDER RETIRE OR RESIGN?

Yes. Paul knew that he was nearing the end of his life when he said, "I have run the race. I have fought the good fight." He wasn't retiring. He just knew he was going home soon.

Truthfully, no one retires from Christian service. We work until God takes us to *his* house. However, it is fine and sometimes necessary for a man to retire as elder. While he will continue his Christian service after retiring from his elder position, he will not have the responsibility, duties, or authority of the position.

In fact, it is beneficial to have former elders in the congregation. Former elders provide support for the team they just left. They help show the congregation how to dwell together in unity even when they are not in leadership. They will always have their God-given talents and the same character (assuming they walk circumspectly). They will not always have their position of leadership.

In circumstances where an elder is in poor health or needs a new job to support his family and the church cannot meet these needs, he should retire. If he still has children at home and needs more time with them, he should retire. That is why young men should not be elders. Managing their households well is a requirement for the office of elder, and raising kids in this culture is not a part-time job.

If an elder is getting very old and there are other qualified men who have demonstrated their ability to take his place, he could retire. Other examples are when he and his family move to another town, or when he is sent out by the church as an evangelist, missionary, or apostle.

Sometimes, a man will lose the fire or motivation for the job. This could be the Holy Spirit leading him to some other work of which he is not now aware. It may be easier to move in a new direction if he resigns the job of elder. Sometimes a man loses the fire when God is revealing sin in his life or is pruning him for greater service and maturity. Regardless, if he doesn't want to do the job, he should resign after counseling with his brother elders. The work is too important and requires too much energy to attempt it by just going through the motions.

One last reason to resign is when one elder is so out of step with the other elders that agreement is not possible. I experienced this very sad situation myself. As I stated elsewhere, I never wanted to be "the Pastor." I wanted to be an elder and serve the church with other like-minded men, using the gifts of teaching, preaching, counseling, and leadership that the Lord has given me. However, our eldership was only a rubber-stamp sounding board for the Pastor. We did not have a collective vision or even seriously discuss issues that the Pastor had no interest in.

As I mentioned in an earlier chapter, I persevered with these men, whom I respect, for many years. Finally, I felt the freedom to leave the eldership. Since they were not going to change, I had become a distraction to them. I asked them to dissolve the eldership and call it what it was: a Pastor's committee. At least then it would be a more honest representation for the congregation. I felt it would be better to have a good Pastor-run church than a poor elder-led church. They would not do as I asked.

Rather than split the baby by discussing this issue with the church at large, I resigned. Like my other friend who found that his gifts were not needed, I left this church after thirty-five years. My family and I visited other churches, and for the last five years we have enjoyed the fellowship and opportunity to serve in a Pastor-led denominational church, where their walk is more consistent with their talk. There is a time for everything.[259]

SHOULD AN ELDER BE FIRED?

A functioning eldership prevents unwarranted attacks on other elders and at the same time provides accountability for each elder. Paul said not to "entertain" an accusation about an elder without at least two witnesses. That does not mean an elder should be insulated from valid accusations, however.

> Do not rebuke an older man harshly, but exhort him as if he were your father.[260]
> Do not entertain an accusation against an elder unless it is brought by two or three witnesses. But those elders who are sinning you are to reprove before everyone, so that the others may take warning. I charge you, in the sight of God and Christ Jesus and the elect angels, to keep these instructions without partiality, and to do nothing out of favoritism.[261]

If a man abuses his wife or family and the other elders have examined the evidence based on two or more witnesses, the elders should

---

259 Eccl 3:1.
260 1 Tm 5:1.
261 1 Tm 5:19–21.

remove him from office. If he abandons his wife or children or if he divorces his wife, except for infidelity, he should be removed. If he commits acts of sexual immorality, becomes addicted to drugs or alcohol, embezzles or steals money, lies, cheats on his taxes, or otherwise breaks the law, he must be fired. These disqualify him based on the requirements of not being a drunkard and not being greedy along with the requirement to be above reproach and held in high regard by those in the community.

When elders take unpopular stands, there will be those who bring false accusations. The standards of proof Paul requires are the same as the Jewish law required. In fact, they are very similar to our own legal standards. Elders must still be wary of the character of those bringing the accusations. Even Jesus was accused by two witnesses in his "trial" before the Sanhedrin. The Sanhedrin was looking for witnesses against Jesus so they could put him to death. Paul exhorts Timothy and the elders to "keep these instructions without partiality, and to do nothing out of favoritism." If the elders are convinced that an elder is continuing in sin, they must deal with it.

I don't use euphemisms. They are dishonest, and most times people see through them. That's why I say an elder should be "fired" if he violates the requirements of the job. The church should not be told he was reassigned to another position or given a sabbatical if that is not true. I have worked in government my entire career. Many times, rather than fire a poor administrator, management will reassign him or her to avoid the issue. Likewise, a sabbatical has nothing to do with discipline; it is a deserved time of rest for a weary elder who will return to his duties at a specified future date. Regardless, if the reason for replacing an elder is not clear, people may think the issue is worse than it is. That hurts the elder, the eldership, and the congregation. We must speak the truth in love.

The discipline for the office of elder is stricter than it is for the average church member. That's one reason an accusation must be proved by factual evidence provided by more than one witness. Though Paul told the Corinthians to expel from their fellowship a man who was sleeping with his father's wife, he was gladly welcomed back to fellowship after his repentance.[262] Had he been an elder, I do not think Paul would have reinstated him, because he had brought reproach upon the name of Jesus in the community, the local church, and the eldership.

This has nothing to do with forgiveness and restoration. It has to do with the consequences of sin and the example set in the church, especially for young people and for the community of nonbelievers.

Remember the commandment, "Thou shalt not take the Lord's name in vain"? God places a high priority on the use of his name and on the character of those who represent his name. In his letter to the Romans, Paul quotes the prophets Isaiah and Ezekiel concerning the contempt other nations had for God's name because of the actions of this people.

> You who boast in the law, do you dishonor God by breaking the law. As it is written: "God's name is blasphemed among the Gentiles because of you." [263]

Hypocrisy is the first thing critics seize upon. If it exists, we should change our walk to match our talk. Otherwise, we are using the Lord's name in vain.

For example, if a worship leader is known to be living with his girlfriend, and the elders do not remove him or otherwise deal with the issue, they are sending a terrible message to all who know. This is especially destructive to young people. All of us make mistakes, but I'm talking about a lifestyle that is well known, and those involved are unrepentant. If the elders do nothing, they are guilty of participating in the sin and defaming the name of Christ in the church and the community.

The issue here is not forgiveness, for all have sinned and will sin. Forgiveness and mercy is granted by the Father to each man and woman

262 2 Cor 2:5–11.
263 Rom 2:23–24

based on our confession and repentance. Jesus's payment for us is acceptable to the everlasting Judge. The issue here is maintaining a high standard for God's leaders. That is why James said let not many of you be teachers for "we who teach will be judged more strictly."[264] One of the most important duties of an elder is to teach the church. God has promised us forgiveness for our sins and salvation from their eternal consequences; but he did not promise an exemption from the earthly consequences.

Even our secular laws require certain moral standards for our elected and appointed officials to hold office. How does it look to us when they flagrantly violate their oaths of office without consequence? It makes a mockery of the law and the office and shows they respect neither the law, the office, nor us. This is one reason we have such a low opinion of elected officials.

Recently, a district attorney from a populous Texas county was convicted of driving drunk. She had an extremely high level of alcohol in her blood. She was even seen on video verbally abusing the jailers and threatening them with her position. Although some tried to have her removed, the courts would not allow it. She continues to preside over the prosecution of drunk-driving cases. What kind of message is that?

The standard for the people of God must be higher than that for our politicians. We should clean house when it is needed and restore to fellowship those who repent, but not necessarily to a leadership position they forfeited by their actions. This will uphold the integrity of God's name in the church and in the community, instill confidence in the leadership of the church, and serve as a warning.

One final word on this issue: the integrity, confidence, and stature of the eldership will be compromised if the elders do not tell the people as much as they can about why they are firing an elder. Paul told Timothy "those elders who are sinning, you are to reprove before everyone, so that the others may take warning." This statement is unclear as to who should "reprove" and who "everyone" is. In chapter 3, Paul says, "I am

---

264 Jas 3:1.

writing you these instructions so that, if I am delayed, you will know how people ought to conduct themselves in God's household...."

I do not think Paul intended that Timothy, as the apostle's representative, or the elders themselves should air all the dirty laundry publicly or slander the person or, by implication, others. This requires wisdom, love, and great care. This is where the shepherd's heart must prevail. If he is willing, it may be preferable for the elder to admit his failure in general terms and ask for the members' forgiveness. If not, another elder should explain the events in general terms. However, it must contain enough detail so that "others may take warning."

There are a number of reasons for making this general information known:

1. The people must know that this was not a false or petty accusation. It was on the basis of two or more credible witnesses.
2. Without knowing the truth, people's minds run wild and gossip spreads. Sometimes knowing what it wasn't is more important than knowing what the failure was.
3. It shows that the eldership is willing to discipline one of its own.
4. It is a warning to elders. Being an overseer of God's people is serious business.

Therefore, a simple and general yet accurate explanation is due to the congregation. It not only protects the eldership, it also protects the persons involved and the church at large.

A TIME FOR STAYING AND A TIME FOR LEAVING

As I have said over and over in this book, we must all submit to one another out of love and respect for our Lord. That requirement also applies to the Pastor, if he is willing to step down and serve as a fellow elder. Each elder must accept his role, share what God has shown him, and defend it in the arena of ideas; otherwise, he is not needed.

Elders are human, just as husbands and fathers are human. Paul said this so well in 1 Corinthians 13 when he said that in this life at best we see through a dark glass. This is all the more reason to have a group of committed men leading God's church. After spending the better part of five years trying to get my fellow elders to understand their roles, I had to be willing to be wrong. In fact, there was a time when I wanted to return to the days where I simply believed and followed whatever the Pastor said because, just like the children of Israel, I wanted to be like everyone else.

Elders must also be willing to allow other elders to be wrong and still stay committed to them. After I shared my ideas with the elders in my church and they did not accept them, I remained active. I did not resign or try to subvert the other church activities. I attempted to serve in ways that were still available to me. These opportunities were limited, however, because my gifts tended to fall into those traditionally reserved for the Pastor, such as teaching, preaching, administration, and vision. So I concentrated on other activities. For example, I helped establish a tuition collection program for our church school (this would usually be a duty of the deacons). The elders were willing for me to do this, and it was successful.

One day, I was walking and talking with a Christian brother who had seen my struggle. He told me I was like Eleazar (one of David's three mighty men), who slew so many Philistines that his hand grew tired and froze to his sword.[265] His point was that I was incapable of letting go of this eldership issue. I assured him I would gladly relinquish the sword when I was sure I had done everything God wanted me to do to convince my brothers. When that time finally came, I dropped the sword willingly instead of splitting the baby with it. I never looked back.

I knew the fight I was picking. I was willing to be wrong, and that is why I waited seventeen years to write this book. I wanted to be certain that I still believed in what I am writing after a long time of watching and "pondering." I still think churches should be pastored and overseen by local elders, with no elder having a higher title than the others.

---

265   2 Sm 23:9–10.

Section 8—How Do We Get There?

THE CURRENT MODEL CANNOT BE reformed. It must be replaced. The Pastor will have to adopt the attitude of John the Baptist. *He must increase; but I must decrease.* The Pastor must resign his position. This is unnatural. It is supernatural. In some cases, the Pastor may have to leave the congregation. In others, he may just step down. In still others, he could remain as an elder. This last option requires more change than the other two, but it can be done. Of course, the Pastor must be qualified to be an elder.

Everything must change when transitioning to an elder-led church. You cannot put new wine in old wineskins. Symbols are very important. The church's *brand* must reflect the new persona. This includes signs, brochures, Websites, and so on. More importantly, the worship service will reflect the change.

As in the first century, the elder-led form of church government is better suited to the days ahead. The current assault on Christians will continue in the United States. We are quickly becoming like other nations.

Elders must be vigilant. If they don't take their responsibility seriously and participate in groupthink, they can make dumb mistakes. If they don't discipline each other, they lose their credibility.

Jesus, Paul, Peter, John, and Jude warned about false teachers and encouraged believers to *contend for the faith*. Elders must not become complacent. When men give up their responsibility, they also lose their authority and privilege.

CHAPTER 26

Revolution, Not Reformation

❦

During my time in England, we moved from London to Surrey and eventually to Eton on Thames. Eton College is just across the footbridge from Windsor Castle, home of the Queen. As one of the kingdom's most exclusive prep schools, Eton has educated nineteen prime ministers and most recently Prince William and Prince Harry. Its sports fields are legendary. When we first drove onto High Street, all the students and teachers were outside. Students were dressed in black tuxedos with white shirts and ties, and the teachers wore capes. This was a once-a-week occurrence they called Confab. We were impressed and felt a bit like country bumpkins visiting the town for the first time.

Every time we drove from Eton to London or other parts of the country, we passed through Runnymede, the site of the signing of the Magna Carta. Feudal barons surrounded King John in 1215 and forced him to sign this document, which provided certain protections to "freemen." However, it provided more benefit to the barons than to the common man.

Over half a millennium later, our founding fathers wrote the Declaration of Independence in Philadelphia. Their declaration of independence from King George of England challenged the idea that any king had a divine right to impose his will by restricting the inalienable rights granted by God to all men.

227

Neither King John nor King George agreed to relinquish control willingly. Both were forced into agreement after exhausting their military options.

Furthermore, the assertions in the Declaration of Independence did not accrue to American slaves. It wasn't until the Civil War that American slaves were granted Constitutional rights as citizens of the United States, and it wasn't until the 1960s that African Americans got full voting rights and other civil rights under the law. In fact, some churches misinterpreted scripture to justify slavery. Without exception, these victories required the sacrifice of blood and treasure to secure God-given rights.

I'm sure there are many social scientists who have studied how change occurs in society. I don't intend to explore their research or recount their findings, even if they support what I say here. Following are my own observations based on my interest in government, leadership, and my personal experiences as a leader and elder.

Most organizations, cultures, and institutions do not change unless forced to do so by outside influence. Some people teach that change is good. I don't agree.

Good change is good and bad change is bad.

There are things God has worked in us that we should preserve and not change. Some are lessons we learned through trials and difficulties. These are experiences that are worth a million dollars to us but ones that we wouldn't pay a nickel to go through again.

In the Old Testament, the Israelites planted boundary stones to mark the land allotted by God to each tribe, family, and clan. The Lord said that it was an abomination to move these stones.

God has taught us holy lessons, establishing boundaries in our lives that we should not trespass. There are other rules and practices we have established as if they were the Word of God, yet they are nothing more than traditions. Jesus himself was constantly accused by the Pharisees of violating God's laws, when in fact he was only violating *their* traditions. He accused the Pharisees of teaching the traditions of men as if they were the Word of God.

Many of the Pharisees' traditions were in opposition to God's will and Word. Jesus pointed out one clear example. The Pharisees loved money, and so they established a practice of having people pledge a portion of their inheritance to the temple. However, if a member of a man's household later had a need (usually his mother or father); the Pharisees would not free the man from his temple pledge and allow him to use the money to help his family member. Jesus pointed out how the Pharisees regarded the temple pledge (a tradition of man) more highly than the fifth commandment to honor thy father and mother.[266] Honor implies more than just respect, it means caring for your parents physically and financially in their old age if necessary.[267]

To become more like Jesus, we must change. One way is to tear down the idols of men's traditions that oppose God's Word. Martin Luther opposed the selling of indulgences for sins by nailing the Ninety-Five Theses to the door of the All Saints Church (Castle Church) in Wittenberg, Saxony. He was credited with reviving the truth of God's Word that salvation is by faith and not by works (or in this case, money).

Though not as profound as the issue of salvation by faith, leadership of God's church is profound. The prevailing tradition of one senior Pastor serving as priest and ruler gives believers and nonbelievers the entirely wrong impression of God's family. In fact, it doesn't even speak of family. It resembles the same hierarchical structure that Jesus attributes to the secular world. This is a tradition of men that must be overthrown and replaced by God's own plan. It cannot be "reformed" by merely adding a rubber-stamp eldership or board of directors. This makes things worse by giving a false appearance and adding more bureaucracy.

There are many reasons that people and particularly leaders resist change. The most obvious are insecurity in leadership, self-promotion, self-preservation, and, in a few cases, honest ignorance. It is to the latter that I write this appeal. The former will continue to defend the status quo.

---

266 Ex 20:12.
267 Mt 15:3–9.

Listen then to what the parable of the sower means:

When anyone hears the message about the kingdom and does not understand it, the evil one comes and snatches away what was sown in his heart. This is the seed sown along the path.
    The one who received the seed that fell on rocky places is the man who hears the word and at once receives it with joy. But since he has no root, he lasts only a short time. When trouble or persecution comes because of the word, he quickly falls away.
    The one who received the seed that fell among the thorns is the man who hears the word, but the worries of this life and the deceitfulness of wealth choke it, making it unfruitful.
    But the one who received the seed that fell on good soil is the man who hears the word and understands it. He produces a crop, yielding a hundred, sixty or thirty times what was sown.[268]

Jesus's parable is not about the seed. This is a parable about different types of soil: how people receive the same good seed (the Word of God) differently.

1. The first type of soil is like a person who is physically able to hear, but this new message cannot penetrate even his intellectual understanding, because he is so disinterested and caught up in his own paradigm. The enemy snatches away the message before it can penetrate the soil and germinate.
2. The second soil represents a man or woman who understands and even rejoices after hearing the message but has no commitment to the truth. Basically, these people are fearful when persecution arises. I think many people fall into this category. How much is the cost of committing to the truth?
        The more profound the truth, the higher the price of commitment. Remember how Paul encountered opposition not only

---

268 Mt 13:18–23.

from the Jews but also Jewish believers for teaching that the Gentiles should not be forced to obey the laws of Moses. Even Peter wavered under pressure from the Judaizers. Likewise, Martin Luther encountered persecution for reviving the truth of "salvation by faith."

One of the worst was in England, where translators of the Bible into English were burned at the stake. This was because the church hierarchy believed that only priests could properly interpret God's Word for the laity (nonclergy). More than anything, this was self-preservation by the church hierarchy. They were afraid that when the people knew God's Word, they would see *his* freedom and no longer tolerate the commands and traditions of man.

The most profound truth is Jesus himself. He said, *I am the Way, the Truth and the Life.* He was infinitely profound and challenging, especially to the Jewish religious leaders. As the price of commitment to Jesus became higher and higher, his followers began to leave him and fall away. We all can identify with Peter, who stayed with Jesus longer than anyone except for John, ultimately denying him three times.

3. The third soil represents people who hear the message but have too much invested in this world to receive it and act upon it. They have encumbered their lives with cares for titles, positions, wealth, ease, and other pleasures. Instead of esteeming God's Word of truth by giving it the highest place in their order of priorities, they bow to the idols of ease, comfort, and wealth. They commit idolatry by choosing these worldly pleasures instead of God's message.

4. The fourth soil is those who have decided to follow Jesus no matter what the cost. They are like the man in another of Jesus's parables who found a great truth (the pearl of great price) and sold everything he had in order to purchase that truth.[269]

---

269 Mt 13:44–45.

In my opinion, each of us will be in various stages of receptiveness (soil types) at various times in our lives. By God's grace, we dare to listen to his Word, understand it, and commit to it regardless of the price. Ultimately, this changes our inward priorities by tearing down idols and traditions of men that prevent it from having a place of preeminence in our hearts.

What Does This Have to Do with Eldership in God's Church?

For the reasons mentioned above, most Pastors, many lay leaders, and many churchgoers will reject this message. It is a fundamental challenge to the status quo, and they are unreceptive to thoughts outside their frame of reference. They don't want to think outside the box even if it really is "inside" God's box.

Many are of the second soil type. At first, they will acknowledge that a clear reading of God's Word shows that the current role of Pastor is not right. They will even get excited about this new understanding. Yet when influential Pastors and scholars begin to refute and challenge this message, they will fall away because they have no "root." They will not have the intellectual honesty and scholarly integrity that the Bereans had when they searched the Jewish scriptures. In so doing, the Bereans found that Paul's "radical" gospel of Jesus had been foretold by their own prophets.[270]

Those Pastors and associate Pastors who have too much invested in the current structure cannot sell all that they have to purchase the pearl of great price. Instead, they will hang their head like the rich, young ruler and return to "their" congregation.[271] Some will even feel like they will be abandoning their sheep if they turn them over to elders.

---

270 Acts 17:11.
271 Lk 18:18–29.

However, there will be those who are of the fourth soil type who have never heard of and understood this teaching before. They are honestly ignorant and therefore are not guilty of rejecting the truth. They will respond and produce fruit. At first, they may challenge this message, and they should. Once they see that the Word of God is clear and that the current role of Pastor is not what God intended for *his* church, they will become the most outspoken advocates for change. Many will be Pastors themselves; others will be lay leaders. Still others, who have never been involved in church leadership because they didn't think the current structure was right, will join in.

Unfortunately, at first there will be very few churches that change willingly. Most existing churches will not change, and the real change will occur outside their doors.

GO TO THE HIGHWAYS AND BYWAYS AND COMPEL THEM TO COME IN

Scripture chronicles how God goes to his people first to proclaim his Word. He gives them a chance to receive his revelation, repent, and change. If they don't receive it, he shakes the dust off his sandals and moves to the next town. In the 1970s, that next "town" was populated by the hippies and unchurched people of my generation.

For example, in the 1970s, the Charismatic movement was rejected by mainline denominations, and therefore, small, disorganized but highly motivated Christians started their own churches where they could worship God in freedom of expression. They also tried out the supernatural gifts that the New Testament clearly says are for the church today.

The Charismatic renewal came about primarily outside the mainline churches. I lived through it. As a young Methodist, I realized that my church was not going to allow the new wine of profound freedoms to be exercised in the old wineskins of a traditional denominational hierarchy.

About the time Charismatic churches were being formed, rock musicians were getting saved. They formed bands to spread the Word in the way they knew best. I was the leader of one of the first Christian rock bands. At first, mainline churches, and even many Charismatic churches, would not allow us to play in church. So we went to the highways and byways to compel nonbelievers to come in. (For more about my experiences during this time, see Appendix A—Liberation Suite.)

Charismatic churches of the '70s were underfunded, lacked experienced leadership, and were definite outcasts from respectable church circles. Yet today they are the establishment of the twenty-first century. They are the most influential evangelicals. Their style of worship, the emphasis on strict belief in the Word of God and belief in the power of the Holy Spirit, are their hallmarks.

Years later, many mainline denominations, in an effort to maintain relevance with today's churchgoer, have adopted some characteristics of Charismatic churches. They added small groups and contemporary music, and they even allowed their people to raise their hands in worship. Most of these, however, still have a problem with speaking in tongues and manifesting other "gifts of the Spirit."

The success and viability of the Charismatic movement and Christian rock began to force mainline churches to accept some of the truths they revealed. I say *force* because they were facing decreasing membership and loss of their most motivated members to these upstart churches.

Am I saying that churches should accept something just because it is popular? Obviously not. What I am advocating will not be popular for a long time, if ever. Whether it is the American pioneers pushing westward or the Charismatic churches and Christian rock bands of the early '70s, pioneers rarely receive the reward of their sacrifice.

Pioneers pay the price. It usually takes one or more generations to see the fruit. Today, Christian "artists" who are as well known as we were earn millions of dollars. We never earned anything, except the favor of God and man and the knowledge that we answered the call. That is the same reward Jesus offers today. There is nothing more fulfilling than hearing the voice of the Father say, "This is my son in whom I am well pleased."

THERE ARE NO HALF MEASURES
(THERE IS NO REFORMATION)

King George tried to placate our Founding Fathers with certain "concessions" in order to bring them back into submission, much like King John had done half a millennium earlier. You cannot have a monarchy and a democracy; just as Jesus said you cannot serve two masters. Although Britain appears to be a democratic monarchy, in reality it's a democracy with a figurehead monarchy. Even the Queen's budget is established by Parliament. Other countries are just the opposite. For example, some monarchies have elections, but the decisions of the elected houses can be overturned by the monarchy. They are monarchies. This issue was discussed in further detail in chapter 22.

The Pastor of our former church told me that the issue of leadership by a single Pastor or a group of elders is a continuum. He believes that neither leadership by one Pastor nor by a group of elders is right. He felt that the answer was somewhere along that continuum. I disagree. They are entirely different animals. You can dress-up the Pastor-led church with an elder board; but if it quacks like a duck, it's still a duck. You either have one or the other.

I am writing this chapter and this book primarily for those who have experienced the Charismatic renewal as I have and now find their church leadership structures to be old wineskins. Although my church started out as a true eldership-led church, it slowly changed to become a Pastor-run church with one figurehead elder.

THE SLIPPERY SLOPE

It is too easy to slide into the familiar leadership structure of the world. But as you see in chapter 19, we are called to a higher calling. We should ordain a group of men who have learned to rule their own households well and are thus qualified to lead God's household as elders.

This will be a supernatural undertaking; yet it is one that God calls his church to achieve. He will bring it to pass if we have faith. However, faith without works is dead. I believe, as in most renewals, the establishment will reject and refute it. Some will try to co-opt it by assimilating it into the existing Pastor structure, as my former church has. That will render it ineffective and a mockery of God's intention for elders.

Some who believe this message will leave their churches and form other churches. I do not think this is the best outcome. I want to see God's people respond to his revelation. I pray that Pastors will lay down their pride and their burdens and work as brother elders or resign from leadership altogether for a period of time and be refreshed.

Unfortunately, most change happens when we are forced into it. Jesus, in his Great Commission, told his disciples to make disciples of all nations, starting in Judea, then Samaria, and then the whole world. Up until the stoning of Stephen, most believers remained in Jerusalem. After the stoning, there was persecution of believers in Jerusalem. This forced many to disperse to other regions and take the gospel with them. *God's will is accomplished one way or the other.*

America is no longer a Christian nation. Soon, the megachurches and other elaborate church organizations will no longer exist or will lose their viability. In some parts of the world, as in the days of the former Soviet Union, believers meet in small groups. When that happens here, we will be in need of the eldership model more than ever. Then, when an elder is arrested or otherwise unable to lead, other elders will provide the continuity of leadership and pastoral care. Do you really think it can't happen in America?

CHAPTER 27

What Must Change?

❧

I attended the wedding of a friend of mine. It was John's second marriage. A couple of years prior, he and his first wife had moved from
East Texas to San Antonio to be near his family. I hired his wife to work
with us because she was a CPA and had many years of experience as a
county auditor. Within a year, she was diagnosed with cancer of the kid-
neys and died not long after.

John and I became friends because we had some things in common.
He and I both loved to hunt. When my son left for his first tour of duty as
a platoon leader in Afghanistan, John and I reminisced about his time
with the 82nd Airborne. So when John said he was going to marry a girl
he had known from high school, I was invited to the wedding.

The wedding ceremony was held in a rural area, in a beautiful garden. John asked his Pastor from East Texas, who had performed his first
wife's funeral, to share his joy by performing his wedding ceremony.
This Pastor was a genuine Texan from Nacogdoches who quickly won
me over with his simple wisdom.

The Pastor looked at John and Elizabeth and said to John, "Do you
plan to go through with this till you die?" John said yes, and I know
he meant it, because I saw how he had cared for his first wife during
her illness. Then the cowboy Pastor looked at Elizabeth and asked her
the same question. Before she could answer, he told them both that
breaking vows to each other is bad enough, but breaking vows to God
is serious. He went on to say that if either of them didn't plan to follow

through on their commitment, then he could just stop the ceremony now and the guests could go eat the food and enjoy the party. Elizabeth assured him that she would live with John for the rest of her life. Then we all went to the reception.

THE PRICE OF CHANGE

Jesus said that a man should count the cost before embarking on an important endeavor. This is applicable to transition from Pastor rule to oversight by an eldership. There are no halfway measures. You cannot put new wine in old wineskins.

> Suppose one of you wants to build a tower. Will he not first sit down and estimate the cost to see if he has enough money to complete it? For if he lays the foundation and is not able to finish it, everyone who sees it will ridicule him, saying, 'This fellow began to build and was not able to finish.'[272]

EVERYONE MUST CHANGE.

The reason we have this unscriptural Pastor role is because Christian men centuries ago relinquished their roles and responsibilities. When the children of Israel stood before God on the mountain, they preferred to send Moses to hear God and tell them what he said. That way, they could question whether Moses really heard from God when they didn't want to follow his direction. Many congregations today just replace their Pastor with a new Pastor who will give them what they want. This is much easier than accepting responsibility for their own leadership.

As discussed earlier, there are Pastors who have gladly accepted their roles because they like to be in the spotlight. Others have a more altruistic motive. They lead because no one else will or because being

---

272 Lk 14:28–30.

"The Pastor" is the only way to use their gift. Don't get me wrong. Not all men and women are meant to be leaders; but all are to hear from God.

In every community, God calls men to qualify themselves for the offices of elder and deacon. As the congregation grows, so will the eldership.

There are a number of ways that a church can transition to eldership oversight. The easiest and best of these is to start the church with this structure from the beginning. However, the title of this chapter implies that we are addressing how a church with a traditional Pastor can *transform* to elder oversight.

THE TRADITIONAL PASTOR ROLE MUST BE ABANDONED.

I started to say the Pastor role must be *replaced,* but in reality, it is such a huge change in thinking that *abandoned* is a better word. Many people think we are abandoning God by eliminating the traditional Pastor role. In fact, as I explained in "Pastor-Priest" and "Pastor-King," starting with Adam, then Israel, and now his church, God's desire has always been for a closer relationship with his people. This Pastor role is an impediment to that close relationship. The correct way to handle impediments to fellowship with God is to eliminate them with a resolute determination. Anything less is a Pastor-led church masquerading as leadership by elders, which is worse than an unapologetic Pastor-led church.

In my discussion of the Kingston church, I noted how the senior elder refused to allow church members to elevate him to a role above the other elders. He and others had come out of the Church of England and knew well the dangers of the religious hierarchy. That does not change the fact that certain elders have more experience and wisdom. That is something I discussed in the concept of "first among equals" in chapter 25.

In the late 1990s, our church experienced a transition from one Pastor to the next. At the time, I was close to the old Pastor and was acquainted with the new one. I trusted and respected them both. I considered both men to be humble and thought this was a great opportunity to see the reestablishment of true elder oversight in our congregation. I spent many hours writing letters and discussing this with both men. I was, however, more than a bit naïve. My old Pastor was not. Looking back, I think he was humoring me. I wish now that he had spoken to me as a wise father and told me the facts of life regarding Pastors. At that time I was unaware how ingrained the Pastor mentality is. I did not understand the Pastors' Club.

Pastors expect their role to be absolute and unquestioned. It is a brotherhood built on common experiences, joys, and trials. They are like noblemen in feudal Europe. Each respects the others' domain. It is the unwritten rule that if I respect your authority you will respect and uphold mine.

Had I known this dynamic about the Pastor's Club, I would have saved all of us a lot of time and energy. I did not realize that neither man would even consider establishing an elder-led church. I described in detail to both how I hoped that the new Pastor and the old one would remain as elders in our church along with the rest of the elders. I envisioned the new Pastor fulfilling the full-time professional duties "assigned" to him by the elders. No one ever said no to these ideas. Yet neither did they say yes.

It was only after the old Pastor announced his resignation and later his leaving of the church that I began to understand. I pleaded with him to stay and explained how his presence was needed to transition those who had close ties with him and show solidarity with the new eldership.

He told me that in order to establish himself, the new Pastor needed no obstacles. He claimed that his mere presence in the congregation, much less his inclusion as an elder, would be an obstacle. I understood that would be true if we were talking about a traditional Pastor role, but I knew that it would be less true if we were reestablishing elder oversight.

I was caught unaware. Had I known we were hiring a traditional Pastor, I would have continued to interview other men who had more of the traditional Pastor qualities. Instead we found ourselves somewhere in no-man's-land between Pastor rule and elder oversight, never achieving the benefits of either. In reality we had Pastor rule with a board of advisors.

The Pastor must be convinced in his heart that elder oversight is God's plan. Once convinced, the Pastor must then decide whether he can be an elder without obstructing the change process. In many cases, this will not be possible.

Just as my church elders all turned to see what the Pastor thought before voicing their opinions, so will new elders if the "old" Pastor serves as an elder. Although, the "old" Pastor may be elder material, in some ways he will be disqualified if only because he represents his former role to the other elders and the congregation. This is sad, and since I believe in a supernatural God, I refuse to believe that this cannot be overcome. It will take faith on the part of the Pastor, elders, and congregation. As Jesus said, "according to your faith so be it."

The old Pastor will have to fully embrace the attitude of John the Baptist. When speaking of Jesus, John said, "He must become greater; I must become less."[273] John the Baptist knew that the one to come was God's Salvation; John was only preparing the way. John was imprisoned shortly after the beginning of Jesus's public ministry. Did God allow this to help people transition from John to Jesus? I don't know. It may have helped, but some of John's disciples had already begun to follow Jesus. Jesus was the fulfillment and the substance of John's message of salvation through repentance.

If the old Pastor cannot adopt John's attitude, he must resign as elder. A single Pastor can talk about living together as the Body of Christ, but as we saw in chapter 5, his very role prevents the fulfillment of that reality. The Pastor must become less so that the other elders can become greater. Only God can do this. In some cases, the old Pastor may need to find another congregation, because the people will continue to try to put him in his old role.

---

273 Jn 3:30.

The old Pastor does not have to leave. If he chooses to stay, however, it will take great effort on his part. It would be better for the old Pastor to remain. If he truly believes the role he previously occupied was not right and can commit to the other elders in a relationship of mutual submission, he can be the greatest example of change. Each time he is tempted to revert to his old role, he must submit to the others out of love and respect. (See the Kingston church example.) When some of his supporters try to restore him to the "throne," he can do as Jesus did when his supporters wanted to make him king by force. He can *withdraw* from them. That act alone will make the message and example clearer than any new elder can.

A congregation and its leaders must have complete commitment to eldership oversight; otherwise, they will never achieve it. Whether the former Pastor stays or goes is dependent first upon his motivation and second upon the faith and resoluteness of the leaders and the congregation.

THE BRAND MUST CHANGE

Many churches follow the latest trends in commercial practices to help promote new programs, manage their finances, draw in new members, or develop their leaders. One such commercial theory is called *branding*. To bring about true elder leadership in a church, not only do personnel need to change; so does the church brand. What is the meaning of branding?

For purposes of this book, the church's brand is communicated through signs, advertisements, bulletins, billboards, websites, brochures, and any other "public" documents. Also included are public announcements, representation on community boards, and interchurch activities such as outreach, training, concerts, and worship services. All of these speak to the church's brand, or its community persona.

These are the questions that businesses ask. What is our brand? What sets us apart? What makes us unique? Businesses live by the positive recognition of—or die by the anonymity of—their product brand. For example, the government-owned auto giant British Leyland was as bloated and as bad as the rest of the British government, but the individual brands of Jaguar and Land Rover were still regarded with high value around the world. These brands will likely continue to have value regardless who owns them.

Branding is important, but what is the church's brand? Most churches, if not on their billboards, have large portraits of their Pastor and his wife on their bulletin boards. The Pastor is the *face* of the church's brand. That is why it is so important for the Pastor to be presentable to the community. Nothing is wrong with being presentable, of course, but what are we presenting? Should it not be the Body of Christ, and not one man? Even though the Body of Christ is espoused by today's Pastors, it is not represented in our public persona or our brand. That is why we must change our bulletins, billboards, and all the rest of our public representation.

Simple things reflect your true image, such as: who is on the payroll, who sits up front during services, whose picture is on the billboard, who speaks at community events, and whose picture is in the church hallway and the church directory.

Part of the mission of an elder-led church should be to educate the community about the nature of the Body of Christ through our different leadership structure. Though changing the brand can be a superficial change, we should strive to make it a representation of who we are: God's people living together in mutual respect, working together for the common good.

Therefore, when the mayor invites community Pastors to a prayer breakfast (hopefully that will happen), the elder-led church sends one of its elders, who is suited for that function. Likewise, in other public roles, such as representing church opposition in the community to immoral activities or participating in interchurch outreaches, the church may send other elders as representatives. Of course, this will cause some confusion at first among community leaders and other Pastors, but as your church grows in favor with God and man, you will begin to present to your community a more accurate representation of the Body of Christ.

When important written communications are necessary, let them come from different elders according to their area of gifting and expertise, with the signatures of all the other elders. Then and only then will the congregation know that a letter from one elder is a letter from *all* the elders.

THE WORSHIP SERVICE MAY CHANGE

More important than anything else is the worship service. It is the purest expression of how the church relates to itself, to God, and to outsiders.

Other than in some small group meetings, the Kingston church is the only place I have seen the type of service Paul mentions in 1 Corinthians 14:

> What then shall we say, brothers and sisters? When you come together, each of you has a hymn, or a word of instruction, a revelation, a tongue or an interpretation. Everything must be done so that the church may be built up. If anyone speaks in a tongue, two—or at the most three—should speak, one at a time, and someone must interpret. If there is no interpreter, the speaker should keep quiet in the church and speak to himself and to God.
>
> Two or three prophets should speak, and the others should weigh carefully what is said. And if a revelation comes to someone who is sitting down, the first speaker should stop. For you can all prophesy in turn so that everyone may be instructed and encouraged. The spirits of prophets are subject to the control of prophets. For God is not a God of disorder but of peace—as in all the congregations of the Lord's people.[274]

---

274 1 Cor 14:26–33.

Therefore, my brothers and sisters, be eager to prophesy, and do not forbid speaking in tongues. But everything should be done in a fitting and orderly way.[275]

The worship service itself says more about the Body of Christ to outsiders and church members than anything else. The type service Paul describes gives no preference to any man or position—*not even to elders.* I think part of this was a carryover from the Jewish tradition, allowing even visiting worshippers to participate. Remember when Jesus was teaching in the synagogue in Capernaum on the Sabbath?[276] That is where he cast out a demon from a man who called out in a loud voice, "Have you come to destroy us?" Of course, the elders of that synagogue may have thought twice about their "open-mike" policy after Jesus caused such a stir. Guess what? The Son of God and the Holy Spirit continue to cause a stir.

Most traditional churches "grieve the Holy Spirit"[277] by only allowing him to move within the fifty minutes allocated for introductions, announcements, offerings, hymns, special music, prescribed prayers, and a fifteen-minute sermon. Even in many evangelical churches, there is no call to repentance at the end.

The Greek verb translated as *grieve* also means "to *cause* sorrow or great distress." The Holy Spirit rarely plays by our "rules" of worship, and therefore he passes us by if he is not welcome. Many members of these churches prefer the predictability of the length and order of events. The movement of the Holy Spirit can be seen as chaotic. It sometimes makes traditionalists uncomfortable to see heartbroken people crying at the altar in repentance. Yet if we don't see this at least occasionally, what are we doing? If we welcome the Holy Spirit and allow him to move more often in our midst, we will become accustomed to unscheduled songs of praise, unrehearsed prayers of petition, expressions of joy and

275 1 Cor 14:39–40.
276 Lk 4:31–37.
277 Eph 4:30.

thanksgiving, tears of remorse and repentance, and tears of joy. If not, what are we doing?

My family and I now fellowship in a traditional church that has a strict order of service. I love the people, and they love my family. But there is no room for deviation from the script. Consequently, the movement of the Holy Spirit is limited. These people serve the Lord by doing good deeds for others. James would be proud of them. Yet in the service, prayers are said only on cue. There are no spontaneous songs arising from the congregation. I miss that. It is such a moving thing to hear the Holy Spirit begin singing from one corner of the room and listen to the rest of the congregation pick it up. This is a beautiful representation of God's family moving as one with the Holy Spirit as the director.

I also miss the testimonies of the people in the service. This is one of the most powerful and encouraging tools we have in the church.[278] Hearing the stories of saints who have trusted in God and seen his deliverance brings faith to the hearers. For this to happen in my current church, it has to be a scheduled part of the program. Consequently, within the past 5 years, I don't remember hearing one. We have allowed the enemy to cut us off from one of our greatest resources, "the faith of our fathers." Our church in particular is filled with older saints who have been faithful for decades. Many die before I know anything of their experiences.

On the flip side, Charismatics and Pentecostals can "grieve the Holy Spirit" by taking the Lord's name in vain. I don't mean cursing the Lord's name. I'm talking about *using it in vain.* That means speaking for God when you're just saying the first thing that comes into your mind because you want to be heard, or speaking out of turn in a meeting. It's sort of like the know-it-all kid in class who wants to answer every question so he can show how smart he is. Give me a break!

Just because you know something doesn't mean it is the right time to say it in a meeting. In fact, it may not need to be said at all. It may be off the topic that the Holy Spirit has established at that point. This is why

---

278 Rv 12:11.

Paul said "The spirits of prophets are subject to the control of prophets." Some of these "prophets" think if they preface their statement with, "Thus saith the Lord," they have established their credibility. Quite the contrary—I consider it a weighty matter to say, "God told me to tell you this." I generally view someone who starts off that way with skeptical caution; even if it is a person I know and trust.

I have been part of a church where unknown people from out of town were allowed to give a prophecy or a word in the service. As an elder, I considered that "open-mike" policy to be generally irresponsible of the Pastor. Even Paul recommended that two or at the most three should share, and the others *should weigh carefully what is said.* Elders are responsible for teaching and refuting false doctrine. Therefore, if a person has spoken something publicly that is misleading to new believers, one of the elders should respond with a clarification or correction. That is the "risk" one takes in speaking without advance notice. In our Charismatic church, a person would normally share the Word with the pastor or one of the elders before speaking.

Although this type of service can at times be messy, it is worth the effort. Families are messy sometimes. But that's why we have grandparents, mothers, fathers, aunts, uncles, and even older brothers and sisters to guide the younger ones. Many times as the church matures, we won't even need to correct the words of a young man or woman in the service. The church as a whole will be mature enough to discriminate between the "word of man" and "the Word of God." Then those "word of man" moments can and should be handled in a private teaching moment. That way the young person (either young in age or a new convert) will not have his spirit crushed and will be encouraged to share again as the Spirit moves him. Remember that our Lord at the age of thirteen confounded the teachers and scribes in the temple by the depth of his questions.

Finally, if people are willing to allow the Holy Spirit to move with freedom in their service, they should be commended. There will be mistakes and errors along the way, much the same as a child learning to walk or ride a bicycle. Just because you bump your head a time or two are you going to say, "I will never try to walk again"? How ridiculous! We who believe in the Holy Spirit–filled life (this includes *all* believers), should have no other goal for our worship service than to make the Holy Spirit of Christ welcome. This rarely happens when one man prepares and directs the order of service.

ELDERS, TOO, CAN GET IN THE WAY OF GOD.

> Then people brought little children to Jesus for him to place his hands on them and pray for them. But the disciples rebuked them.
>
> Jesus said, "Let the little children come to me, and do not hinder them, for the kingdom of heaven belongs to such as these." When he had placed his hands on them, he went on from there.[279]

Even a well-meaning group of elders can get it wrong sometimes. The disciples still didn't fully understand the heart of the Father. It was for these "little children" that he sent his Son. I expect this was the last time the disciples prevented someone from coming to Jesus.

Hopefully, humble elders with a willingness to submit to the perspective of the others and to the Holy Spirit will learn to guide others to Jesus rather than prohibit them. Then all will participate in a worship experience that is truly "heavenly."

---

279 Mt 19:13–15.

CHAPTER 28

The Days Ahead

❧

Most societies throughout the world that oppose Christianity do not have large, Bible-teaching churches. For example, during the Soviet reign, large churches existed, but they were dominated by the government. Their hierarchy was approved by the government, and their teaching was censored. This article from the London *Telegraph* (2014) shows that things in China aren't any different today:

> Communist Party officials have rejected claims they have launched an orchestrated campaign to slow the spread of Christianity in China, after demolition teams razed a church in a city known as the "Jerusalem of the East."
>
> The Sanjiang church in Wenzhou, a wealthy coastal city in Zhejiang province with one of China's largest Christian populations, was reduced to rubble on Monday night....
>
> China could be set to become the world's largest Christian congregation by 2030, a leading expert told the Telegraph earlier this month. Monday's demolition sent a chill through China's Christian community, now thought to number anywhere between 23 million and 100 million people. Some church leaders and academics fear Beijing may be paving the way for a nationwide campaign targeting the officially illegal "house

church" movement that refuses to accept Communist Party oversight.[280]

These are the trials the church in the first century faced in Jerusalem and other Roman cities. Our brothers in the Soviet Union, China, and in Muslim countries face the same thing today. How did they survive? Better yet, *how do they thrive?* Almost without exception, they survive in "house churches."

We continue to build church edifices and infrastructure that will only survive in a government atmosphere that protects our Constitutional and God-given rights to freedom of worship. Those days are numbered in America. In Scandinavia, it is already a crime to preach from the Bible about homosexuality. Hate crime laws in America are not far behind. We are already seeing local governments trying to preview or subpoena sermons.[281]

Jesus said that we will not know the hour or the day when he returns; but he implies that we should be able to interpret the signs of the times. Jesus replied to the Pharisees and Sadducees, who asked him to show them a sign from heaven, by saying,

> "When evening comes, you say, 'It will be fair weather, for the sky is red,' and in the morning, 'Today it will be stormy, for the sky is red and overcast.' You know how to interpret the appearance of the sky, but you cannot interpret the signs of the times."[282]

The signs are clear. Even nonbelievers can interpret them; but those who claim to hear from God are ignoring the signs.

---

280 http://www.telegraph.co.uk/news/worldnews/asia/china/10794749/China-denies-declaring-war-on-Christians-after-mega-church-is-razed.html (Accessed February 11, 2015).

281 http://www.houstonchronicle.com/news/politics/houston/article/City-subpoenas-sermons-in-ERO-court-case-5822800.php (accessed February 10, 2015).

282 Mt 16:1–3.

It Can and Will Happen in America.

Our church leaders act as if our churches will be able to continue in their current form for decades. Some see it coming but don't know what to do. Others don't know any other way. Worst of all, others don't acknowledge the coming storm because they don't want to give up their position. This last group will fit right into the Soviet-style churches because all they want is to be in charge of something.

During the time of Jeremiah, the Jews believed that God was obligated to protect them because *his* temple (*his* house) was in Jerusalem. They believed this even though they worshipped false gods in *his* house and burned their children as sacrifices to the demon-god Molech. Jeremiah attempted to straighten them out on this point. He told them that the Lord would destroy *his* temple (which the Babylonians did). He reminded them that many years earlier the Lord had already allowed *his* resting place at Shiloh to be overtaken by the Philistines who captured the Ark of the Covenant for a period of time.[283] This also was because of the sin of Israel.

Similarly, Jesus prophesied the destruction of the second temple in Jerusalem (which the Romans did). While in the temple, Jesus pronounced seven woes on the teachers and Pharisees saying, their house would be left to them desolate. As he left, he said that one stone would not be left on another. Though the Jews no longer worshipped idols, this could have been God's punishment for rejecting his son, the Messiah. Jesus said, "You will not see me again until you say, 'Blessed is he who comes in the name of the Lord.'"[284]

If the Lord is willing to destroy temples built by *his* chosen people to honor *his* name, why do we think that our existing church structures and organizations will fare any better?

God is not obligated to uphold our tax deductions for charitable giving. He doesn't care if our church buildings are exempt from property tax. He is not overly concerned about us continuing to have unfettered

---

283 Jer 7.
284 Mt 23–24:2.

access to air our programs on the radio and television. His focus is on how we govern his household and how we spread the Good News of the gospel.

> As long as it is day, we must do the work of him who sent me. Night is coming, when no one can work.[285]

Our Window of Opportunity Is Narrow and Short.

The sun will soon set on some of the privileges mentioned above. We are facing a persecution never imagined in the land of liberty. Free speech will no longer include the ability to preach from the Bible. Though the Good News of salvation and good works are preached, the mere suggestion that there is an eternal judgment of sin will not be tolerated. Hate speech laws will make it a crime to oppose certain "alternative" lifestyles, such as homosexuality, and to preach about God's judgment. It follows that no savior is needed if there is no sin and no judgment. We will find ourselves gathered in homes praying for our brothers in prison, like the disciples in Jerusalem prayed for Peter's deliverance from prison. He was jailed for preaching the gospel.[286]

If any of this rings true in your heart, you must admit that the time for our current church structures is nearing an end. These require such vast amounts of administration, overhead, and reliance on tax-deductible gifts that they will no longer survive. Neither will the small churches on every corner. They also have vast amounts of overhead in comparison to their total church budget and attendance.

Let us work while it is still day and prepare to manage God's household in a more viable, efficient, and yes, more scriptural manner.

---

285 Jn 9:4.
286 Acts 12.

CHAPTER 29

A Final Word to Elders

૯ઝિ૦

Most courts interpret laws by applying a *plain reading* test. That means the court first interprets a particular statute based on how a normal adult with reasonable intelligence would interpret the written law. The whole reason I have written this book is because a plain reading of the New Testament clearly provides that the local church is to be governed by elders. To make a case for Pastor rule requires a tortured twisting and turning of scriptures, which clearly refer only to elders.

The New Testament provides no bishop or other church official to oversee the local elders and their churches.[287] The glue that held certain churches together in the New Testament were the apostles who started each church. Even so, Paul, as the founding apostle of the church in Corinth, did not claim sole oversight. He encouraged the apostle Apollos to go to Corinth as soon as he could to help them.[288]

I planted the seed, Apollos watered it, but God has been making it grow.[289]

I have made the case for returning to the New Testament model of church government. It should be local and limited. No matter how "excellent" the model of government is, it must be administered by

---

287 The Greek word translated *bishop* is the same word used for *elder*.
288 1 Cor 16:12.
289 1 Cor 3:6.

men who adhere to the intent of those who established the model. Our Constitution, our Bill of Rights, and our Declaration of Independence are only as good as the paper on which they are written, unless free men with courage and conviction adhere to and defend those principles with unwavering commitment. So it is with God's institutions.

As with the Constitution of the United States, there are those who say the New Testament eldership model was for an earlier period, and that model no longer works in today's society. They say that church government must change with the times. This is similar to the debate we are having between strict constructionists and those espousing a living (changing with the times) interpretation of the Constitution. Some Supreme Court justices have gone so far as to interpret our Constitution by referring to laws of the international community. This is clearly an attempt "to be like other nations." Similarly, Christian teaching for centuries has taught models of church government that resemble those of secular society, whether it is a corporation or a political government.

The Children of Israel wanted to be like other nations, and they suffered the fate of other nations. They went into captivity until they renounced the idols of the other nations and remembered the one true God. Likewise, many of our "leaders" in America downplay the uniqueness of the "great American experiment" and seek to be like other nations. We are fast becoming like other nations and may not recover the amazing results of freedom that our "experiment" has provided.

The form of church government instituted by the apostles was not the only form of government from which to choose. Paul, Peter, James, John, or Apollos could easily have adopted the Roman or Greek forms of government...or made up something different. However, the Lord himself told them not to treat each other like the Gentiles by lording it over each other.

This book is a call to return to the New Testament form of church leadership. We cannot accrue the benefits of the elder model without the courage and commitment of individual elders and other men in the church to see it accomplished and maintained.

- *It is easier* to default to a CEO Pastor to get things done more quickly.
- *It is easier* to hire a priest to tell us what God wants us to do than to ask him ourselves and be responsible for the answer.
- And yes, *it is easier* to go along with the crowd and not stand alone. Therefore, we hire a Pastor-king to represent us.

God has called us to be a holy people, a royal priesthood, to be different from the other nations.[290] He calls us his "elect." If God elects us, how can we refuse his higher calling?

The hardest part of establishing a true eldership is not the transition from Pastor rule to an eldership or the immense task of replacing false concepts with biblical concepts. It is the constant vigilance and teaching required to keep the people and the elders from "returning to Egypt."

When our "New Testament Church" started in 1973, it was much more like the elder-led model than it is now. Then, we ordained one of the elders as Pastor. That was the first thing we did wrong. We should not have given one elder a different title than the others. Later, we began hiring Pastors from outside the church and automatically giving them the title of elder. Giving the new Pastor a title of elder was merely to perpetuate the myth that we were an elder-led church. By this time, the Pastor ran the show. It is very easy to slide back into a Pastor-dominated church; especially if the elders are lazy and refuse to do their work.

I think it is right to give "double honor" to those elders who labor well in teaching and preaching. The idea of *honor* as Paul described it carries with it the connotation of financial support. A church may support a number of elders financially, but they should never be given a title or position superior to the other elders.

The problem with supporting one elder financially to the exclusion of the others is a temptation to recreate a clergy/laity division. This can be avoided by a careful division of responsibilities in accordance with the talents of each elder and the time they can dedicate. When the church

---

290   1 Pt 2:9.

sees only one man in the church office during the week available for counseling, and that same man as the only one teaching and preaching, he will become a de facto Pastor. This is especially tempting when that one man is the only one with a seminary degree. It may be better to partially fund more than one elder to be available during the work week. Of course, this requires each man to be able to make up the difference in a part-time job elsewhere. The apostle Paul was a tent-maker. In places where he felt the people would think he was preaching and teaching for the money, he refused to take their money and supported himself completely. Men who are retired may be better able to fill this role of elder.

All elders should be able to teach the Word and refute false doctrine. This is one of the primary requirements to be an elder. Therefore, they should be doing this as much as they have time to commit. They should also be available as much as they can to provide counseling. Some people will be drawn to one elder in particular, and that is how it should be.

If one elder shows a significant gift for preaching and teaching, the elders should consider providing more financial support so he can spend more time performing those duties. He need not have a seminary degree if his teaching is sound.

It is more likely that the elders, rather than the people, will be sucked back into a de facto Pastor-run church. This is particularly true because the commitment of time and energy to be a functioning elder is immense. That's why it is important that each elder be aware of the time commitment required before accepting an appointment. No matter how good a candidate appears, elders must not appoint a gifted man who does not have the time or has family issues that he needs to tend to.

Each elder must work diligently within the realm of his authority as delegated by the eldership. This is the best defense against allowing a de facto Pastor to arise. Likewise, the eldership should give each elder who has a teaching or a Word from God the time to preach or teach, as needed. The same elder should not always have the prime time on Sunday morning or Wednesday night. If one elder is the most gifted in preaching or teaching, you would expect him to have more opportunities than the others; but all should be able to exercise their gifts. This is an extremely important visual sign to the church, and it provides the diverse perspectives that are essential to knowing a diverse God.

Elders should police themselves. If they see that a man has too many personal and family needs, they should counsel him to take a "sabbatical." This is not to be confused with a resignation. If it is obvious he needs more than a few weeks or months, he should probably resign and the elders should seek a qualified replacement, because there is work to be done. If he desires to return, let the elders decide. It is good to have former elders in the congregation. It strengthens the eldership, especially if the resignation was handled properly.

In other cases, a man should resign if he has committed a sin that disqualifies him. This does not mean that he is not to be forgiven, but he may have to forfeit his position of leadership in order to protect the integrity of the office and provide an example to others. Too many Pastors have been restored to the ministry after having affairs. I'm not saying it should never happen. I'm saying it happens too often, and the message to the people is that it doesn't really matter. Betraying the trust of God, your fellow elders, your church, and young people who look to you as a mentor, *matters greatly.*

The following sections are prefaced by quotes from Proverbs chapter 27. There are many notable quotes in Proverbs, but this chapter is a good one for elders to remember.

Speaking the Truth in Love

Wounds from a friend can be trusted, but an enemy multiplies kisses.

As iron sharpens iron, so one person sharpens another.[291]

---

291 Prv 27:6, 17.

There is no room for yes-men on the eldership. We cannot have elders who turn their heads to see what the Pastor thinks before expressing their own opinion. We need independent thinkers. Some of the most secure, confident men are the quietest. They should not be quiet in the eldership. Obviously, they don't have to be the first to speak, but they must be heard at the right time. The time to speak is when all voices have been heard and the consensus decision is terribly wrong. That is the time an elder must be the lone voice crying in the wilderness. If it is really important, he must not compromise. He must stand firm. Only then will he be able to rein in the rush commitment decided by groupthink.

The commitment of the elders to one another and the understanding of love and respect between them should be able to withstand the sharp disagreements that will occur over important matters as they each "speak the truth in love."

Constant Reflection and Humility

The crucible for silver and the furnace for gold, but people are tested by their praise.[292]

I was a high school senior and a college student during the early development of our New Testament Church. I regarded our eldership at that time with respect and a little fear. That was probably more about my insecurity than their autocratic style; however, I do remember thinking that their decisions were like a decision from God. The church as a whole perpetuated this impression.

As I grew older, I came to hear teachings that I questioned, such as those espousing extreme discipleship and the prosperity doctrine. Later, even the elders began to leave these doctrines.

My warning to elders is to not believe your own press.

---

292 Prv 27:21.

- You are not as wise as you think.
- You are not as stupid as some people think you are.
- You are not immune to groupthink.

You can make some really stupid decisions. When you do, you should repent of them publicly and ask forgiveness of the congregation if necessary. Wise folks already know it was stupid; they just want to know that *you know* and that you are concerned about the harm you caused.

CONSTANT VIGILANCE

> Be sure you know the condition of your flocks, give careful attention to your herds;[293]

The definition of *groupthink* focuses on the concern the "in-group" (elders) has for itself, rather than concern for the "out-group" (the congregation). I titled this book *The Pastors' Club* because I saw how local Pastors relate to each other as an exclusive club or guild. I don't want to have to write another book about the *Elders' Club*.

The whole purpose of the eldership as Jesus commissioned Peter is to "feed and care for his sheep." Elders are to pastor *(poimen)*, shepherd. They are to lay down their lives for the sheep. Their concern should always be for the good of the people and not themselves.

Israel's prophets, by the Spirit of God, pronounced woes on Israel's faithless shepherds:

> "Woe to the shepherds who are destroying and scattering the sheep of my pasture!" declares the LORD.[294]

---

293 Prv 27:23.
294 Jer 23:1.

Woe to you shepherds of Israel who only take care of yourselves!
Should not shepherds take care of the flock?[295]
Woe to the worthless shepherd, who deserts the flock![296]

Jesus pronounced seven woes on the Pharisees and teachers of the
law. He accused them of being hypocrites and using their position to
better themselves without concern for those they were charged with caring for.[297]

A FINAL WORD TO THE CHURCH
The writer of Hebrews said it best:

Have confidence in your leaders and submit to their authority,
because they keep watch over you as those who must give an
account. Do this so that their work will be a joy, not a burden, for
that would be of no benefit to you.[298]

---

295 Ez 34:2.
296 Zec 11:17.
297 Mt 23.
298 Heb 13:17.

Appendixes

Appendix A—Liberation Suite

∞

IN 1974, OUR BAND, LIBERATION Suite, moved from Texas to Belfast, Northern Ireland, to preach the gospel. Northern Ireland is a province of Great Britain, with its own provincial parliament. The southern Republic of Ireland still claims Northern Ireland as part of its Republic. Consequently, when we landed in Dublin in May, the Irish immigration officials detained us, saying we had no visa for Ireland. They did not buy our explanation that we were just passing through on our way to Northern Ireland. So we missed our connecting flight and took the train up to Belfast the next day.

I remember standing in that deserted, bombed-out train station in Belfast watching British troops patrolling with automatic weapons. We had arrived at the height of the Protestant workers strike during "The Troubles." This was one of the worst times for sectarian violence between the Catholic minority and the Protestant majority in this British province.

The entire province of Northern Ireland was shut down by the Protestant Ulster Defense Force (UDF).[299] Their goal was to prove that they, not the Catholic Irish Republican Army (IRA), ran the country. British troops and the Royal Ulster Constabulary were caught in the middle. If businesses tried to open, the UDF would blow them up. If cars tried to run the blockades, the UDF would seize and burn them. It

---

299 The UDF was the Protestant answer to the Catholic IRA (Irish Republican Army).

was a dark rainy day, standing alone in that bombed-out train station. We were relieved when our car, driven by nurses, picked us up and took us through the blockade to Cottonmount House in the countryside.[300]

We were young and naive. It had not really occurred to us that religion *was the problem* here. Both sides were very religious. I remember spending the first night thinking, *these people have a lot of important things to worry about. What if they don't like rock music?* But the method and the message we brought transcended these boundaries in a remarkable six-month period. God knew that these young people loved music and that Northern Ireland didn't have many bands traveling there during the Troubles.

The next six months was one of the most important periods of our lives. Even though It wasn't unusual to hear bombs explode in Belfast and see cars on fire when returning from a "gig," we played constantly in every major city center across the province. All centers were blocked off for fear of car bombs. With only one exception, officials allowed our band of long-haired rockers from Texas to set up in their town centers. It was not unusual to have a crowd of one thousand kids come to listen to us play, preach, and give our testimonies. We then invited them to give their lives to Jesus and join us at area churches.

Though we were never invited to play at Catholic churches, we did play to many Catholic kids at these impromptu concerts. The city centers in Northern Ireland were considered "safe zones" during the day for Protestants and Catholics.

We also played in Dublin and other cities in the predominantly Catholic Republic of Ireland. On one trip, we played in Newry, an IRA stronghold near the border. As we approached the border, we passed a British checkpoint with a heavily fortified concrete bunker. It was covered with netting to prevent bombs from being tossed on top. Once we reached Newry, we played downtown right after an IRA rally. One of the Catholic young men invited us home to meet his family. We had a great

---

300 Nurses are revered in Northern Ireland; otherwise they would not have been able to get to us.

time, but I noticed that one of our young Protestant companions sat terribly silent the whole time we were there. Later, he told us this was his first time in a Catholic's home. I guess he thought he might be killed if they found out he was Protestant.

During our stay in Northern Ireland, we played in schools, bars, large concert halls, and even dance venues where the Rolling Stones had played. Later in England, we played at large outdoor festivals. We had many open doors to use rock music to preach the gospel. There were quite a few Christian bands and artists starting up in England. We played with many of them, but we were one of the very few that preached the gospel. Too many of these groups wanted to be stars. One did eventually have a hit record.

Our goal was to preach the gospel and see the lost saved. We conducted altar calls at each concert, except those where we could not. It was not uncommon to see as many as forty or more young people accept Jesus as their savior at the end of our concerts. We prayed with them and led them to repentance and salvation. God moved mightily, and we still hear of the young kids from those concerts—who now are parents and grandparents. Using a worldly method may work if you have the right message and do not alter it. We offered something different and genuine, and they knew it when they heard it. The delivery method was something that the kids would listen to when the churches couldn't reach them.

In 1974, while still in Ireland, we were invited to play the first Greenbelt Festival in England, where thousands of young people heard the message of God's love through our music and preaching. Also present were representatives of Word Record's new contemporary label, Myrrh. Soon afterward, we signed with Myrrh, moved to London, and recorded our first album in Wimbledon. This brought us even more open doors. Eventually, the band moved to Surrey, where it met the church in Kingston and then on to Eton near Windsor.

Churches and youth groups throughout England, Scotland, and Wales began to book us. We played colleges, schools, prisons, and small outdoor events. We played major venues in Belfast, Dublin, Rotterdam, Essen, Helsinki, Goteborg, and Oslo. We played the Royal Albert Hall in London with Larry Norman and a theater near Piccadilly with Barry McGuire. We toured Scandinavia, England, and Ireland with Chuck Girard of Love Song. We recorded in Abbey Road studios and were asked to play on Cliff Richard's TV show.

We always played for suggested donations, and the Lord provided for us even though we were traveling with eighteen people. Christian rock was in its infancy and was still viewed with a certain amount of skepticism and opposition. Yet we met many Christians, young and old, who had a desire to spread God's Word in a new way in the United Kingdom.

Eventually, churches began to see how effective we were and they began to sponsor us to play citywide concerts for their youth ministry. They also helped us get permission to play in schools and prisons. The doors were wide-open to us in Britain.

After the success of our European and Scandinavian tours, we set our sights on Europe. At that time, the "Iron Curtain" was still a cruel reality. We had become friends with a Yugoslavian performer, who was arranging for us to tour his country. From there, I expected we would foray into Poland and other Communist Bloc countries.[301] However, this was not to happen.

With the stress of three married families and inexperienced leadership, the band began to break up. This was a time of severe anguish for me. I had given up a promising future in the United States and had never planned to return. God had supported our ministry in so many ways when the odds were stacked against us. Why was he pulling the rug out from under us when the doors appeared wide open in Europe and maybe behind the "Curtain?" I thought maybe God knew we weren't mature enough to handle the popularity (our

---

301 At this point, certain Bloc countries began scheduling rock bands. I thought this was a tremendous opportunity for us to bring the gospel behind the "Curtain" to young people.

concerts in Germany and the Netherlands were very well attended). I also knew that Britain had many churches for those who accepted Jesus at our concerts. Most of Western Europe and countries under Communist control did not. We were evangelists. We were not teachers or pastors. We could not provide a home or family for those who were "newly born" believers. God would have to provide that in other ways.

I remember feeling like Moses must have felt when God took him up to Mount Pisgah to look at the Promised Land just before he died.[302] He could see it but he was not to go there. I really thought our next step was behind the "Iron Curtain." However, I only got to see it from a distance.

Even though some of the band members wanted to go their own way, I really felt abandoned *by God*. I remember looking out the window of the plane as I left London on my way to Texas. I even remember the song by Eric Carmen that was playing on the intercom. Finally, the following words came to my mind as clearly as if I had heard them. "The sooner you learn what I have for you in the United States, the sooner you will return."

To be honest, it has been forty years since I left England and I don't know if I will ever return. I do know that those words gave me closure and a new mission. I went back to my parents' home, finished college, and became a CPA. I had always wanted to be a good husband and father and now that I wasn't on the mission field, I felt the freedom to look for a woman who would love me and share my love for God. I thank God that these were *his* plans for me as well. Daryl and I have been married thirty-two years and we are sending the youngest of our four children to college this year. This book is my first, but maybe not my last. I hope to share more of what God has taught me in these last forty years.

---

302 Dt 3:23-29

Editorial Review by Randy Brandt
(February 18, 2003) for Al Menconi Ministries

"Liberation Suite," produced by British artist/producer, John Pantry, was originally released by Word Records on the Myrrh label in 1975. Recorded at R.G. Jones Studio, Wimbledon, England, November 11, 1974 through December 12, 1974, "Liberation Suite" quickly became a classic, and was nominated as one of the top three releases in a reader's poll conducted by Britain's Buzz Magazine. REVIEWS Two decades before the O. C. Supertones or Five Iron Frenzy, a rock band with a horn section burst onto the Christian music scene. Liberation Suite's self-titled debut from 1975 caught my attention from the opening cymbals on Led to Roam. I'd never heard anything quite like it. The songs were flavored with blues, a touch of country, a little jazz, and plenty of rock. The horns were certainly unique, but not too many Christian bands in 1975 had Barry Bynum's raw rock guitar sound, either. Besides that, what could be cooler than a band of long-haired Texans without cowboy hats, and with two pairs of brothers (Howard and Paul Lyon, Barry and David Bynum), not to mention a drummer (Randy Hill) with my first name? ...The album holds up well a quarter century after it was recorded in England by this young (teens and early 20s) but talented band that had relocated from Texas to Ireland. Everyone in the band sang, provided unusual harmonies for a rock band, and only Phil Keaggy's Glass Harp managed to utilize the flute and electric guitar in the same songs with the success of Lib Suite tracks like Led to Roam and Run Run Lucifer. This is truly an eclectic project musically, but the lyrics consistently proclaim Jesus Christ as the sole (soul?) remedy to life's problems. That message must have come through clearly at their live shows as well--popular recording artist Benny Hester became a Christian at one of their concerts.

Liberation Suite – No Rock in Church

Original Promo - 1972

Liberation Suite – Cornmarket, Belfast, Northern Ireland, 1974

Liberation Suite – Rotterdam, The Netherlands, 1975

R.G. Jones Studio, Wimbledon, England, December 1974

Sunday Best in Eton, 1976.

Liberation Suite – 1976

Scandanavian Tour with Chuck Girard, 1976

Appendix B—All the King's Horses

⬦

BEFORE THE PEOPLE OF ISRAEL entered the Promised Land, God told Moses that they would one day reject him as king and appoint their own king. This happened over three hundred years later when the people asked Samuel the prophet to anoint a king so they "could be like other nations."

God told Moses to give the people the following restrictions and instructions about how Israel's kings must conduct themselves. He also explained the reasons for each.

> When you enter the land the Lord your God is giving you and have taken possession of it and settled in it, and you say, "Let us set a king over us like all the nations around us," be sure to appoint over you a king the Lord your God chooses. He must be from among your fellow Israelites. Do not place a foreigner over you, one who is not an Israelite. The king, moreover, must not acquire great numbers of horses for himself or make the people return to Egypt to get more of them, for the Lord has told you, "You are not to go back that way again." He must not take many wives, or his heart will be led astray. He must not accumulate large amounts of silver and gold.
>
> When he takes the throne of his kingdom, he is to write for himself on a scroll a copy of this law, taken from that of the Levitical priests. It is to be with him, and he is to read it all the days of his life so that he may learn to revere the Lord his God

and follow carefully all the words of this law and these decrees and not consider himself better than his fellow Israelites and turn from the law to the right or to the left. Then he and his descendants will reign a long time over his kingdom in Israel.[303]

We can see that God gave these rules for a reason.

1. Not a foreigner.
He must be from among your own brothers. This requires little comment. He must be family.

2. Not many horses (otherwise the people will return to Egypt).
Horses and chariots represented military might. God did not want his people to rely on the nation of Egypt or any other nation for its protection. He wanted Israel to rely upon him. This required faith. God intended to deliver his people without help from other nations in order not to share his glory with them. Ironically, King David penned the following, even though he also violated the prohibition against acquiring horses and chariots.

Now I know that the LORD saves his anointed; he answers him from his holy heaven with the saving power of his right hand. Some trust in chariots and some in horses, but we trust in the name of the LORD our God. They are brought to their knees and fall, but we rise up and stand firm.[304]

It was especially loathsome to the Lord to have his people return to Egypt (the place of their slavery) for help. Even today, many people say that American warplanes saved Israel during the Yom Kippur war in 1973. God will not share his glory with men. There will be a day soon

---

303 Dt 17:14–20.
304 Ps 20:6–8.

when Israel will not be able to count on help from America. Then the whole world will know that God is her protector.

3. Not many wives (or his heart will be led astray).

God created Adam and Eve as a perfect match. He said it was "good." However, because of man's greed and lust for more, he acquired more wives. Many wives lead the king's heart astray from God. Solomon is an excellent example of this. Even King David's biggest problems resulted from his desire for many wives. His lust for Bathsheba resulted in much heartache for David and hardships for the people he led:

- adultery
- the murder of Bathsheba's husband
- the death of the child of adultery
- the rape of David's daughter by one of his sons
- the murder of that son by another son
- the overthrow of David's kingdom by his son
- the rape of David's wives by his son
- that son's subsequent death

Having children of multiple wives creates competition among the wives and their children for preeminence. This dynamic occurs today when men and women are divorced and have multiple marriages.

4. Not much silver and gold (no stated reason).

Although God gives no stated reason here, we can infer at least two things by reading the text from Samuel's warning to the people when they demanded a king: the king will tax the people, and he will conscript their sons and daughters for his service.[305]

---

305 1 Sm 8:8–17.

How much do we need to say about taxation? In the hands of unaccountable men and women, it is a curse upon the people. Even in America, where we have representative government, taxes are imposed on people by those who do not have to pay them. The more the king wants, the more he will take from the people.

5. Keep a personal copy of the law and read it all the days of his life (so that he will learn to revere the Lord and not consider himself better than his brothers).

This is the one *do* out of the list with four *don'ts*. Knowing the Word of God helps a leader to honor God and prevents him from lording it over his brothers.

This is the essence of Jesus's response when asked about the greatest commandment. Jesus quoted from Deuteronomy and from Leviticus when he said, "Love the Lord your God with all your heart and with all your soul and with all your mind," and "Love your neighbor as yourself."[306] "All the Law and the Prophets hang on these two commandments."[307]

God intended the King to behave like all of his children by respecting God and showing love to his children. The more power a man is granted, the more he needs to read God's Word. It reminds him that he is caring for God's sheep and to God he must answer.

---

306 Dt 6:5, Lv 19:18.
307 Mt 22:37–40.

Appendix C—The Apostle

THE APOSTLE DESERVES DISCUSSION IN another book. I will not expound upon the gift of the apostle, but I must mention it here in relation to the offices of elder and deacon. Apostles have a unique task as overseers in the early stages of the churches they establish. I use the word *have* instead of *had* because apostles are functioning today.

Apostles appoint the first council of elders in a new church. After the church is established, the elders take full responsibility. It's normal that the elders and the church as a whole will continue to respond to and respect the opinions of the apostle, as a son would his father. But once the elders are functioning, the apostle should not assert his authority as a governing official; since that is the elders' role. This is similar to the role I have in guiding my oldest son. He is married and sometimes asks my opinion on matters. However, I have no authority to tell him how to run his household, because he answers to God, not to me.

Apostle literally means "the sent one" or "agent." As an apostle, Paul also calls himself a spiritual father to the churches he established, or "gave birth to." In the same book of Ephesians from which I derive much of the foundation for this book, Paul mentions the role of the apostle in the founding and administration of churches. In the following passage, he speaks to the Gentile church in Ephesus and explains how they are one house of God with the Jewish believers:

Consequently, you are no longer foreigners and aliens, but fellow citizens with God's people and members of God's household, built on the foundation of the apostles and prophets, with Christ Jesus himself as the chief cornerstone.[308]

Surely you have heard about the administration of God's grace that was given to me for you.[309]

Paul's administration of grace (gift and call) to the Gentile churches included

1. defining the qualifications of elders and deacons;
2. appointing the first elders in each church;
3. working with and teaching the elders and the people until they could stand on their own feet;
4. providing continual instruction and oversight through his letters (epistles) and visits by himself and other apostles; and
5. establishing church discipline as in the cases of the Corinthian and Galatian churches.

---

308   Eph 2:19–20.
309   Eph 3:2.

www.ingramcontent.com/pod-product-compliance
Lightning Source LLC
Chambersburg PA
CBHW061424040426
42450CB00007B/896